MW01617218

drawn

together

A Couples Devotional

Inspired by
FamilyLife's Art of Marriage

drawn together

 FamilyLife®

Orlando, Florida

Drawn Together
FamilyLife Publishing®
100 Lake Hart Drive
Orlando, Florida 32832
1-800-FL-TODAY • FamilyLife.com
FLTI, d/b/a FamilyLife®, is a ministry of Cru®

ISBN: 978-1-60200-916-5

Design: Julie Sullivan, Meraki Life Designs
Photography credits: iStock (Kate_sept2004 and Alvarez)

Printed in Canada Through Bookmark

27 26 25 24 23   1 2 3 4 5

🏠 FamilyLife.

Contents

Before you dive in:

Please note that this book was written for marriages where addiction, affairs, or abuse are not involved. These situations require more help than we can offer as a trusted friend here. A good working definition of abuse is a pattern of physical, psychological, and emotional behavior meant to exercise power and control over another person.

If there is any form of abuse in your marriage, separation may be a necessary first step to protect the life of the abused and get the abuser the help he or she needs. But announcing a desire to separate without first having a plan in place can be dangerous. If you are in an abusive situation, contact the National Domestic Violence Hotline for help making a plan. Call 1.800.799.SAFE (7233) or visit https://www.thehotline.org/

Introduction:

Your Marriage, God's Masterpiece

Do you remember the moment you just *knew*?

You *knew* you didn't just want to hang out anymore. You *knew* you wanted more than just dinner and a movie. You *knew* this time ... it was different.

Now think about all the seemingly inconsequential choices that drew you to that moment in history. You chose to walk instead of hopping on the subway. You worked from a different coffee shop that day. You filled in for a coworker. You almost didn't go to that party with your friend. You had no idea when you went to that restaurant, or church, or school, you would run into *her* or *him*.

But in the Christian life, we don't see mere coincidence.

One might say you were *drawn together* by a Celestial Painter who took the canvas of human history and brought your two brush strokes together.

You said, "I do," but God said, "I did."

And "He did" for a purpose. In Genesis 1:27, we read that God created humans to be His image bearers, a word often translated as "icon." Leaders would commission sculptors, painters, and artists to craft "icons" of themselves—visible representations of a leader most people would never see, speak, or hear from in their lifetime. We are, in a way, the graffiti of God, meant to show, speak, and splatter the invisible nature of God to a world that desperately needs to know its Creator.

And yet, if God is truly crafting a work of art in our marriages, most of the time it doesn't feel like a masterpiece. How quickly we went from "I *just knew*," to "I just *never knew* . . ." that you'd need so much "me-time." Or that sarcasm is your second language. Or how hard it would be to say, "I'm sorry." But this Artist doesn't waste the stains and spilled paint produced by our sin. He blends it perfectly with the red streak of His Son's sacrifice. God's masterpieces are not just about living happily ever after.

When Jesus prayed for His disciples in the Upper Room, He revealed the purpose behind God's people becoming One (whether it be a cadre of disciples, a church, or a covenantal marriage), "That *they may all be one, just as you, Father, are in me, and I in you, that they also may be in us, so that the world may believe that you have sent me*" (John 17:21, emphasis added).

Six sections divide this devotional, each with a unique Hebrew or Greek word illustrating the character, quality, or intention of God.

Hesed (Hebrew)

Dabaq (Hebrew)

Agape (Greek)

Luo (Greek)

Yada (Hebrew)

Euangelion (Greek)

As we embody these words toward one another and those around us, two things happen: we are drawn together into the oneness we long for, and others (our kids, stepkids, grandkids, neighbors, and coworkers) are drawn toward God.

Whether your marriage is struggling, barely surviving, or thriving, the Artist can blend every aspect of your marriage into a masterpiece of His glory. Don't give up. Keep moving toward Him and each other. Remember, before you *knew*, God *knew*.

HESED

A half-dozen over-the-top English words only begin to capture this single Hebrew term. Combine *kindness, loyalty, tenderness, faithfulness, mercy,* and s*teadfast love*, and you get the idea. This is an action word. You don't merely talk hesed. You show it. Even more, hesed is a covenantal word, making it unconditional. That's why one of the finest displays of God's hesed love toward us is marriage itself. Our hesed love toward our spouses points the watching world to Jesus' hesed toward His church.

Hesed love doesn't ask, "Have you qualified for my best? Do you deserve my time, attention, and best attitude right now?" It flows like a fountain, boldly disregarding conditions. Drawing deeply from the well of Jesus' own hesed love, we can lavish our spouses with it.

"Are You Guys Getting a Divorce?"

By Tracy Lane

> *Then the Lord God said, "It is not good that the man should be alone; I will make him a helper fit for him."*

GENESIS 2:18

"Are you guys getting a divorce?" Our nine-year-old almost whispered it from the corner of the kitchen.

We hadn't said that word, but her question wasn't a surprise. We had to pause from our three-week-long argument to hear her.

I definitely wasn't going to be the one to say no, because I wasn't sure we weren't right then. I also wasn't about to be the first one to show I was still committed. I really hoped Matt would say no so I could try to believe him. But he didn't answer our daughter's question either, showing me he also wasn't sure right then of the forever state of our marriage.

We'd been stuck in a very tough season in our marriage for about eight years:

- Welcoming our second baby, a daughter with a life-threatening heart condition.

- Moving across the country (and away from our support system) for her medical needs.

- Matt struggling to accept the limitations of his career in a new place.

- A surprise pregnancy ending in a miscarriage.

- And finally, adding a new baby to our family . . . who also had a significant medical diagnosis.

The odds were stacking up against us. And with each one, we felt farther and farther away from happily ever after. We both coped our separate ways and operated in opposing survival modes.

After our silence in response to our daughter's question, I texted a friend who had been mentoring us: "Really this time. There's no way we're going to make it. We couldn't even tell her we're staying together. Because I don't think either of us knows if we are."

We sat at our mentor's kitchen table a few days later and both admitted we *wanted* to want our marriage, even though right then we didn't. We *wanted* to want to keep trying. Even though we didn't know how. So Zoom calls turned into monthly dinners at their house. They listened to us, which meant we finally had to listen to each other. They asked the right questions to help us both understand what we were struggling to trust God (and each other) for.

They believed Matt could lead our family, not just a high school baseball team. So he started trusting God for it. They guided him to step into all the hard details of our family with me—even though choosing his exciting coaching career instead would've been more fun.

To my shock, he said no to a prestigious full-time coaching position he really wanted and any mid-career coach would be crazy to turn down. But we knew from experience that long nights at practice and games five nights a week created an absence in our family that couldn't be made up in a few weekend hours.

Our mentors believed I could trust God and trust Matt for many things I held tight control of, so I started handing them over. They gently guided me to allow Matt the space in our home, even though the learning curve felt too steep for me to loosen the reins. We'd all grown quite accustomed to me over-functioning (the clinical word my counselor used). I needed Matt's help.

We began learning the practical, day-to-day ways to do life together. I could ease his learning curve, and he could start studying. For example, I wasn't going to miss a single dose of our daughter's medicine, and I'd memorized the long list of prescriptions to rattle off in an emergency. Matt asked me to type out that list so he could save it on his phone, and he established phone alarms at her designated medicine times.

As the practical logistics were shared, we started feeling the safety to share our hearts, too. Before, I'd call a friend to vent about something or ask my sister to accompany me to a difficult appointment. Now, Matt was taking sick days off work to ride along to our kids' kidney ultrasounds and blood draws. He researched the new medicine the doctor mentioned. We were sharing all those experiences, feelings, and decisions together.

I wasn't holding the expert card anymore, and he wasn't winning somewhere out there while leaving me with the weight of our home's hardship. Plus, the sheer number of hours we were in all of it together simply added to a feeling of partnership. We were practicing and becoming a true team, exactly what Matt is great at leading.

Back to that question our nine-year-old asked. Neither of us answered her, which brought her no relief that day. But at that moment, what I'm most thankful for is that even though neither of us said no, more importantly, neither of us said yes. We continue to answer that question every day by honoring God with our commitment to His design for our marriage. And our kids are just three of the people experiencing the relief in that.

Draw it out:

1. Can you both say you're sure about the forever state of your marriage? Why or why not?

2. If your answer above is no, what do each of you need from your spouse in order to feel their commitment to your marriage? How can you show your spouse you're in this for the long haul?

Pray together:

Thank God for the gift of a partner to do life with, especially when life is hard. Ask that He would help your marriage feel secure, a safe space for you both to rest when life's demands pull and push. And pray for His strength and resolve to be able to commit yourself to your spouse, not letting "divorce" ever be an option.

The Secret to a Successful Marriage

By Dennis Rainey

Continue steadfastly in prayer, being watchful in it with thanksgiving.

COLOSSIANS 4:2

One of the most important pieces of advice I've ever received was from a mentor of mine, Carl Wilson. I remember going to Carl four or five months into my marriage to Barbara and asking, "What's the best piece of advice you could give a young man like me who is just starting out a marriage?"

Carl put his arm around me and said, "Well, Denny, I would encourage you to pray with your wife every day. No matter what, pray with her."

He seemed to have a good marriage, so I decided to commit to praying together with my wife, too. It sounded simple enough, but I'll tell you, I didn't realize at the time how important it would be in our marriage.

You see, sometimes Barbara and I don't like each other very much. One of us may have said or done something to hurt the other. Maybe one of us is feeling neglected or disrespected. At the end of the day, we're lying in bed—she's facing one way, and I'm facing the other. We're both awake, but no one is talking. Have you been there?

In those moments, the Lord will come to me in my conscience, and He'll say, *Hey, Rainey. Are you going to pray with her?*

I'll respond, "No, Lord, I don't like her tonight. Besides, You know in this situation, she is ninety percent wrong, and I'm only ten percent wrong."

Yeah, but your ten percent caused her to be ninety percent wrong. Pray with her.

I don't like admitting fault. When she's the one who's ninety percent wrong, it doesn't make it any easier. (Often, that's flipped.) When there's something between us, I don't want to go near her. I want to stay as far away from her as possible. The last thing I want to do is pray together. But you know what? Sometimes in marriage, I have to do the thing I don't want to do. I have to take responsibility for my part and follow through on my commitments, even when it's uncomfortable and I don't feel like it.

When a **husband & wife** *pray together* regularly, they invite God to take the lead in their **relationship.**

There were nights it wasn't easy at all. But our commitment to prayer would force us to talk about the issues we were facing. Sometimes we would resolve it fairly quickly; other times, we couldn't. The issue was so big we needed to table it until the next day. But we would still find a way to pray together in some form or fashion, even if it was just a simple, "Lord, we're not together on this tonight, but we acknowledge you, and we want you to still lead us, rule us, and be the Lord of our marriage."

There were also nights our prayer was, "Lord, we're so tired. We love you. Goodnight." That's okay. Praying together doesn't have to be some overly churchy experience. It doesn't have to be big, long, or drawn out. Even a short prayer together reminds us that we don't belong to ourselves. We don't even belong to each other. We belong to God. And by doing that every day, we're inviting Him to be a part of our relationship. We're saying, "We need you, God. We want you to be involved. We need your guidance." When a husband and wife pray together regularly, they invite God to take the lead in their relationship. And when we do that, the trajectory of our marriage changes.

There is a special word for this kind of love in Hebrew. It's called "hesed." It's a love that is steadfast, merciful, and kind. It's love in action, even when difficult. When you have every reason in the world not to love, but you choose to pour out your favor anyway, that's hesed. And I'll tell you, a successful marriage, one that goes the distance, needs that kind of love.

Our daily commitment to prayer has been the best spiritual discipline we have in our marriage relationship. It keeps us connected with God and to each other each day. I'm convinced we wouldn't be married today without it. But thanks to some advice from Carl, we are.

CONTINUE

steadfastly

in prayer, being

WATCHFUL

in it with *thanksgiving.*

COLOSSIANS 4:2

Draw it out:

1. What would you say is the biggest reason keeping you from praying together more often?

2. How do you typically respond to conflict? Do you tend to pull away or pursue restoration?

3. Hesed love is steadfast and long-suffering. Name one way you have seen your spouse express this type of love.

Pray together:

Thank God for His steadfast love for you both, for the ways He has pursued you, even when you were difficult to love. Thank Him for your spouse, and ask Him to fill you with a hesed kind of love. Commit to God and each other to pray regularly in a way that works for you.

Draw closer:

Wondering what FamilyLife's Art of Marriage is all about? Get a preview at FamilyLife.com/DrawnTogetherBonus. And while you're there, take a quick marital assessment to know which areas of your relationship could use the most attention right now.

My Wife. My Love. My Idol.

By Ron Deal

> *They exchanged the truth about God for a lie and*
> *worshiped and served the creature rather than the*
> *Creator, who is blessed forever! Amen.*

ROMANS 1:25

I'll never forget the day I figured out my defensiveness is really me trying to argue my wife into liking me. What a dumb idea.

As if arguing with her about her opinion doesn't infuriate her even more, right? She feels like I'm not hearing her, that I'm just trying to push my agenda. She feels unloved and uncared for. And . . . dare I admit this in print? She's right. (Batting a thousand there, Ron.)

I craved Nan's approval at my core for so many years. So badly, I had to argue with whatever detail or perspective it was, as if it really mattered to get back in her good graces again. The irony is not lost on me.

See, for a lot of years in our marriage, I worshiped something other than God.

The subtlety was the crazy part of it. Aside from the above example, an onlooker might have actually thought I was a stellar husband because of my idol. I mean, I *should* care about how my behavior impacts my wife. And I certainly want to love and serve her as much as I can. But at that time, and many times since, I've made her opinion of me my ultimate compass—rather than who God calls me to be.

Yet I believe and know and trust that when I live up to who God is calling me to be, I am going to be the best for my wife. As I surrender myself in submission to Him, I'm also going to find better ways of loving and serving and giving to my wife.

At last, through the Holy Spirit, it dawned on me: *Wait a minute. God tells me who I am. My wife doesn't tell me who I am.* The truth? In moments where I have Nan's disapproval, God still empowers me to be who He tells me and calls me to be.

If you know anything about idols, their origin story always involves a craving—a desire swelling beyond its proper, legitimate place. Pastor John Piper once authored a poem, "Love Her More and Love Her Less,¹" for the occasion of his son's wedding. He lyrically counsels his son to love his wife more than wealth, friends, ease, and art. But, he counters,

> *Be sure to love her less than God.*
> *It is not wise or kind to call*
> *An idol by sweet names, and fall,*
> *As in humility, before*
> *A likeness of your God.*

Now, seeking to order the loves of my heart, I can actually sit and listen and endure my wife's disapproval long enough to hear her out. Who knows what opportunities will be presented to us when I don't have to try to win her approval right away? It's liberating.

And it actually helped me begin to love her better.

God centers us and our marriages—like clay on a potter's wheel. When He's not the center, everything else starts collapsing on itself.

When I allowed God to move back to center, it also had the beautiful effect of allowing my wife to better manage who she was in that moment. She no longer had to argue with me to prove her point. Instead, she was freed to be her best self.

It's like the wedding ring I gave her. I told her the larger

God
centers

us and our marriages.

diamond in the middle represented God. On each side is a much smaller diamond that represents us. He's what unifies us. His truth orients us to how we live life, and His truth empowers us to love one another. We want to be more like Him, centered in Him. We want Him to be the thing that brings us together.

That's the beauty of God's design. When we put Him in charge of who we are—rather than the other person or the relationship—He becomes both the Potter and the rightful center. And the vessel of our marriage curves into who He's called us to be and He empowers us to love the way He loves.

Draw it out:

1. Examine any dictating desires in your own life—perfection, approval, achievement, comfort, control, etc. In your marriage, how have you witnessed that desire morphing into something you must have?

2. Ask your spouse, "What's it like for you when this desire takes over? What does it rob from you? From us?"

3. Consider a situation when this desire tends to take over—perhaps when you're tired, anxious, or angry. What could it look like for God to reclaim Himself at the center of your soul?

Pray together:

Thank our amazing Creator that He holds all things together (Colossians 1:17). Ask God to wake you up to the ways your desires and insecurities take center stage rather than Him. This week, ask Him to point out when this is happening. And ask Him to pull you back to Him—and all the ways He's enough for what you long for.

Unpacking Your Baggage

By Jonathan "JP" Pokluda

> *Therefore, confess your sins to one another and pray for one another, that you may be healed.*

JAMES 5:16

If the honeymoon is a prelude of what's to come in marriage, then we should have expected a world of hurt. Before we even boarded the plane for our honeymoon in Mexico, I was bruised and profusely bleeding . . . literally. I'm not blaming my wife, but it may have had something to do with all the baggage she had. Let me explain.

After saying, "I do," on our wedding day, we were leaving for a week-long honeymoon. I packed for one week in one suitcase. Monica packed for one week in six suitcases. That's not an exaggeration—six suitcases. So there I am, her new husband, and I'm like, "Hey, I got it. Don't you worry."

We did remote parking at the Dallas/Fort Worth International Airport, and I loaded those seven suitcases onto the bus—my one and her six. Then I unloaded those seven suitcases onto this huge escalator. It was enormous! I'm thinking maybe five-stories high. If you've been there before, you know I'm only slightly exaggerating.

No matter how big it really was, having all those bags gathered up on that escalator made it seem like a monumental feat. I was leading the way, and Monica was behind me. As we got to the very top of that escalator, one of those suitcases caught the side and jerked us backwards. I began to flip, head over heels, all the way down this five-story escalator.

Therefore, *confess*
your sins to one another
& *pray*
for one another, that you may be
healed.

JAMES 5:16

As I flip, I hit Monica, and she begins to flip. Now, as her new husband, who happens to stand six foot seven inches tall, I'm trying to protect her and keep her head from banging up against something. By the time we reach the bottom of that five-story escalator, I'm bruised and bleeding profusely, as I mentioned earlier. And this is how our honeymoon and marriage began. All due to the baggage we brought with us.

That experience was painful, but the metaphorical baggage we brought into marriage has been a lot more painful than those seven suitcases. For me, that baggage came in the form of calling in sick to work so I could stay at home and binge pornography. For others, maybe even you, the baggage might be wounds from a mother or father. Perhaps it's abuse you thought you would never talk about or an abortion you swore you were going to take to your grave. It might be an addiction of some sort—to food, alcohol, drugs, or even spending.

All of these things need to be checked. When brought into marriage, they become stronger, more encompassing. They will drag you down, like our baggage dragged me down that five-story escalator. The difference is, once married, you have someone alongside you. If you aren't careful, you and your spouse may end up painfully flipping head over heels, trying to limit the bruising and bleeding in your marriage.

So, how do you limit—or completely get rid of—the baggage you may have brought into your marriage? You have to open it up and unpack it. You have to reveal what's hidden inside. When you do this, you can then begin the process of healing. Healing reduces and/or eliminates the destructive items, so you can fit in the items that produce the most love, the most joy, and the most peace in your marriage. Then you'll be able to experience the healthy, life-giving, and beautiful marriage God has for you.

There is a kind of

healing

that is only available to you through

prayer & confession.

Throughout the Bible, we're exhorted to live as children of the light and to walk in the light. James 5:16 says, "Confess your sins to one another and pray for one another, that you may be healed." There is a kind of healing that is only available to you through prayer and confession.

I encourage you to open, unpack, and reveal what's inside your suitcases. On the outside, they are probably nice-looking, matching, and well put together. Yet on the inside, they have your unmentionables, your personal items, or just a jumbled mess of everything all thrown together in a hurry. Confess these things to one another, pray together, and begin the process of healing in your marriage.

Draw it out:

1. Separately, make a list of some baggage you either brought into marriage or accumulated during marriage that isn't producing love, joy, or peace in your relationship.

2. What is one thing you are willing to confess, discuss, and pray with your spouse about? Circle it on your list above, and set aside time to pray and discuss.

3. Who can you reach out to for help as a counselor or mediator as you and your spouse unpack this bag in your marriage? Think of someone who loves God, loves you, and loves your spouse. Then ask them to pray for your marriage and to meet, as needed, to help you through this process.

Pray together:

Read James 5:16 together and thank God for the power and privilege of speaking directly to Him. Ask Him to forgive anything you've kept from Him and your spouse. Thank Him for healing and for the amazing journey you're on together in marriage.

The Sweet Spot in Marriage

By Bob Lepine

Oh, magnify the Lord with me, and let us exalt his name together!

PSALM 34:3

I remember the minutes before our wedding ceremony, standing off to the side, waiting for it all to begin. I was thinking, *How do you do this? I mean, how do you know for sure—right here, right now—that this is the one for life?*

Around the time we got married, a song on the radio included the lyric, "It's sad to belong to someone else when the right one comes along." I thought, *What if three weeks from now, I meet somebody and go, "She's the one?"* I had this mini panic attack.

Then the thought hit me, *You do this by faith.* You trust God has brought the two of you together. You trust that she is the one for you, and you are the one for her. There was not another "one" coming along in three weeks, three years, or three decades.

Over the years, I've heard some men say, "Just because I've ordered, it doesn't mean I can't look at the menu." And I've thought to myself, *Why keep looking at the menu if you've already ordered? Are you looking at the menu in case you don't like what you're getting? Are you looking at the menu so you can think, "Next time ..."*

While I came to realize the decision to marry Mary Ann was an act of faith, I didn't necessarily get it right when it came to my view of what real love is. Looking back, I realize now that when we got married, my view of love was, *I love how Mary Ann makes me feel when we're together.* I was making a long-term investment in that feeling. If I'm honest, a big reason why I married Mary Ann was so I could continue to experience the way she made me feel. I had a very self-focused view of love.

Over time, I realized I needed to be thinking not primarily about how she made me feel, but about how I made her feel. I realized I have a responsibility before God to love and cherish my wife and to create an environment where she felt safe and valued. But as important as that is, it's still an incomplete way of thinking about love.

In the end, the essential question isn't, "How does this relationship make either of us feel?" The question is, "Does this relationship please God?" Instead of asking, "Am I happy in our marriage?" or "Is she happy in our marriage?" the more important question is, "What's God's perspective in our marriage?" For all of us, glorifying God with our lives is the ultimate goal. Love is not just other-centered, it's ultimately God-centered. "Whatever you do," the Bible tells us, "whether you eat or drink, do all to the glory of God" (1 Corinthians 10:31). That's our primary assignment. Our chief end.

Psalm 34:3 says, "Magnify the Lord with me, and let us exalt his name together!" A God-centered marriage is a marriage where a husband and wife say, "That's what we're in this for.

We're together not primarily for the benefits that'll accrue. We're in this primarily because we believe that together we can magnify the greatness of God in a way we couldn't if it was just the two of us as individuals."

Only when glorifying God is the centerpiece of our marriage can we say we have a God-centered marriage. This sweet spot is where you want to be. But it doesn't mean everything is going to be simple and easy. Even in a God-centered marriage, you'll experience challenges. So don't be discouraged. But when both of you keep coming back to the ultimate purpose for your marriage, you will experience God's blessing on your union.

Marriage is harder than you think. And it's sweeter than you think. It's going to take work to make it sweeter, but it's worth it to press in and to invest and make it what God intends for it to be, rather than treating it casually and hoping it will all work out. When you find the sweet spot in marriage, where God is truly at the center, it's sweeter than anything you can imagine.

magnify
THE LORD with me...
PSALM 34:3

Draw it out:

1. Do you remember the thoughts you had on your wedding day? Discuss some of these thoughts with your spouse.

2. What thoughts do you have today about marriage or what love is that are profoundly different from your newlywed days?

3. Looking at your marriage today, what do you think God thinks about your marriage? In what ways does it (or could it) "exalt His name"?

Pray together:

Thank God for being the Author and Architect of this sweet gift called marriage. Thank Him for your spouse, who is the one for you (and vice versa). Confess any areas and thoughts you've had that play a part in keeping you from the God-centered marriage He brought you together for. Ask God to show you how to make pleasing Him a priority in your marriage—over focusing on what feels good to you, or even what feels good to your spouse. Then praise Him in advance for making your marriage sweeter than it has ever been.

Marriage Is Rarely What You Expect

By Daniel and Christina Im

> *And let us not grow weary of doing good, for in due season we will reap, if we do not give up.*

GALATIANS 6:9

When it comes to marriage, how often is it what we thought it would be?

I (Christina) thought we'd have lots of sex. And it's been a blessing that our libidos have mostly matched. But I didn't necessarily expect sometimes not even wanting to be in the same room with Daniel. Or times I feel alone. Every intimate relationship has conflict, and our marriage is no different.

Maybe, like us, you thought you were entering marriage with eyes wide open. We had some tough conversations, read some books, and people warned us marriage is hard. We were ready!

But *expecting* something to be hard and *experiencing* something as hard are wildly different things. While we knew on some level we'd have conflict and disappoint each other, that knowledge didn't really protect us from the pain.

Some unmet expectations turn out to be not that big of a deal. For instance, I (Daniel) pictured Christina would play video games with me (and enjoy it!). That one hasn't panned out, but we do find other ways to have fun together. That was the real heart behind my desire anyway.

There have been times for both of us—in the middle of a conflict, or disconnected from each other, or exhausted from life and kids—that we've just wanted to quit. Like Elijah in 1 Kings 19, who was so physically and emotionally exhausted he told God he wanted to die, sometimes the weariness, discouragement, and anger just knock us on our rears. That depressed feeling where our expectations are unmet can distort our view of our marriage. The outlook can feel grim.

Truth is, God's expectations for marriage are different from ours. You remember what the Bible said marriage is a picture of, right? Jesus gave up not only His preferences and comfort, but His *life* for His bride, the church. In response, and with the help of the Holy Spirit, the church serves its Savior with its entire heart, soul, and mind. (Slightly different from a video-game partner and lots of sex.)

God's expectations for marriage

are different from ours.

Though we don't always understand, we've found God's expectations for marriage are far better and more beautiful than ours . . . even though it doesn't always feel good at the moment. But like Jesus, who endured the cross for the joy set before Him (Hebrews 12:2), the richness of the kind of love that "bears all things . . . endures all things" (1 Corinthians 13:7) is worth the daily, difficult choices that nurture it.

Deep down, all of us want more than a conflict-free, fun friend in marriage. We want something even better. *Something better* is what God designed marriage to be—an embodied, tangible experience of God's never-giving-up love. Like God's love, in marriage, we're supposed to be able to experience a person who sees us, knows us best, and also loves and delights in us. Isn't that beautiful? Isn't that worth working toward?

For us, that kind of oneness is made up of countless little choices day by day, week by week, year by year. Choices to put our phones down, close our laptops, and look into each other's eyes for conversation. Choices to be vulnerable and allow ourselves to be fully seen when it would be easier to stay superficial. Choices to sacrifice mindless entertainment in favor of something that brings connection. Choices to forgive and ask for forgiveness more times than we thought we ever could. Choices to lay down our preferences and comfort for the good of our spouse.

To walk in the kind of one-flesh love God intends for us in marriage, it helps the two of us to keep the long view in mind. There may be seasons where we pour ourselves out and see very little fruit of intimacy and connection in return. But because we have God's view of marriage in mind, we don't give up. We continue to do good in the midst of our weariness. How? We draw from the deep well of God's love, who never grows weary of loving us exactly as we are, day in, and day out.

That's a love we can count on and expect.

Draw it out:

1. What are some unmet expectations you've had in marriage?

2. How does knowing God's big picture of marriage change the way you look at your spouse?

Pray together:

Take time to thank God for His perfect love toward you both. Ask Him to help you release your expectations of your spouse and marriage in exchange for "something better." Pray you will be mindful of the day-to-day choices that lead to oneness (or threaten your connection) and for help in choosing wisely.

What to Do about the Person You Thought You'd Marry

By Janel Breitenstein

Many are the plans in the mind of a man, but it is the purpose of the Lord that will stand.

PROVERBS 19:21

Who did you think you'd marry?

A few years into our marriage, when my husband and I finally had the fortitude to be more vulnerable with each other, I unearthed that he thought he'd marry someone more athletic. (I am laughing out loud as I type. Poor guy.) To his credit, when he met me, I was running every morning, performing push-ups and sit-ups at night. We played intramural sports and pickup games of soccer together. We hiked together. To be clear, I remain physically fit, yet painfully unable to walk and chew gum simultaneously.

For my own part, I thought I would marry someone who sang well. (Because music could be called my heart language, I have a Texas-sized soft spot for harmony and acoustic guitars.) My husband laughs that though our college choirs sang in the same concert, we never crossed paths because I was "in the good choir."

When a friend and I chatted about this, she said she thought she'd marry someone who would, along with their dog, go running everywhere with her. In this conversation, her husband snorted. "I got bad news for you, Hon. You not only got the wrong dude. You got the wrong dog." Their Great Dane is essentially motivated by . . . nothing.

So there's definitely a humorous side to this. But there's also pain. As we settle into the reality of marriage—sprouting love handles along with gray hairs the gauge of electrical wire—unmet expectations = loss. Occasionally, we're tempted to look over our shoulders.

But in our extinguished expectations, it's so easy to descend into bitterness, or even a sense of loss or betrayal.

This reminds me of someone's anecdote about their recent trip to a natural foods store for a return. "No problem!" the clerk responded. "If this doesn't fit your narrative in any way, we'll gladly take it back."

Sometimes after marriage, it can be a little too easy to think, *You don't really "fit my narrative." Do you happen to have a generous return policy?*

Truths to keep in mind:

- Our decisions to marry possess gaps. None of us marry for the perfect reasons. But God anticipates this.

- Even your perfect person is not perfect. God is the only one who knows what we will truly need and desire in the long term—not just what would make us comfortable or match our fantasy spouse.

God loves me so much better, so much wiser than I love myself. His dreams supersede my guitar-soundtracked, rapturously harmonized ones. And in the pain of reaching toward each other and enduring dashed hopes, my husband and I have watched real, Velveteen love emerge.

Because what stands in the way of love, so often, is ourselves.

Like Jesus, as we die to our desires and rights and demands, love emerges more alive than ever. "By this we know love," John writes of Jesus, "that He laid down his life for us" (1 John 3:16). He asks us to join Him in death and resurrection, expanding our love in response to His.

When we're tempted to give into resentment or give up, we can choose to believe that God writes our stories on purpose: "The Rock, his work is perfect, for all his ways are justice" (Deuteronomy 32:4). We can be grateful for that real-life, Technicolor love, gray hairs and all.

Even then, I've found He doesn't leave me to fend for myself. His Spirit's sculpting tenacious, tangible love in place of my selfish, grasping pseudo-love.

Love—as a parent, as a spouse—lacks a fire escape. I'm thankful my marriage did not come with a return policy. Nor did my kids. Neither did I come with one when I arrived in my parents' arms. Nor will God ever accuse me of not fitting His narrative.

Another truth: Marriage is sheer faith. But not in your spouse. And not in yourself.

You may be in an exquisitely painful position obscuring why God matched you with this person. Maybe you've become different people. Quite possibly, they're not the person you thought they were. Or maybe you're not the person you thought you were. Even then, marriage is not "I do. Until I'm not happy." Ultimately, your co-signer, your ultimate safety net, is Someone infinitely bigger than the one you married.

Make it your life's work to love well the one you're with. And who knows? You might just stumble upon a love story. With or without a Great Dane or guitar.

Draw it out:

1. In what ways are you now more like God because of the work required by enduring love?

2. What's one season in your life that you're grateful someone persevered in loving you, even though it was probably hard?

3. In your words, how does the lack of a "fire escape" in marriage change a relationship? If you're able to do so sincerely, take a minute to express or reiterate your unconditional commitment to your spouse.

Pray together:

Thank God for never letting us go and for persevering with us unconditionally, because of Jesus. Ask Him to teach you to love each other like this, exposing to your hearts the ways you travel in discontentment, fear, bitterness, or faithlessness. Ask Him to build tenacity and godward trust in your souls.

Your Marriage Is Not beyond Hope

By Crawford and Karen Loritts

> *"What therefore God has joined together, let not man separate."*

MARK 10:9

We've been married for more than fifty years. And I (Crawford) will never forget what my dad said to me on my wedding day, May 22, 1971. As he shook my hand, he whispered in my ear, "You asked Karen to marry you, and you'd better take care of her."

My dad comes from a long line of strong, healthy marriages. I grew up with two parents, who weren't perfect, but loved each other and poured out that love onto their children. My parents were great at modeling respect, working together, and the value of faith in marriage. But when Karen and I got married, we were just twenty and twenty-one years old—kids, really. We soon found out that applying what had been modeled to our own marriage was easier said than done.

Early in our marriage, I (Karen) struggled with knowing who I was as a wife. I knew what the Bible said about marital roles, and I had seen it modeled by Crawford's parents and couples in my church. But I came from a single-parent home and was raised to be self-sufficient by the women in my family. So when disagreements came up about spending money or maybe Crawford made a decision I disagreed with, I didn't know how to approach this agreeably in our marriage. I would end up being a little snarky or just stuff it down and allow those issues to be a barrier between us because I couldn't talk it out.

And all the while, the words of my grandmother were in the back of my mind, "If it doesn't work out, you can always come home."

I (Crawford) had some maturity issues, too. I didn't like anyone telling me what to do, and we both had to deal with my young, out-of-control, male ego. To add to it, neither of us are what you would call "passive" people. We both have very strong personalities, so there have been some choppy waters over the last fifty years.

We've grown and matured, but we still have issues we're working through. All marriages do. But a marriage that lasts involves commitment.

Over the years, we've learned the importance of resolving disagreements by apologizing and working through it together. We have to fight against, "If it doesn't work out..." because there can't be exit signs in marriage. We had made the decision to marry, so Karen and I had to make the choice to stick it out.

I know some people might be reading this and thinking their issues are too big. That their marriage might be beyond hope. But let me tell you, if God can raise a dead Jesus, there's not a problem you have that He cannot address and transform.

Because all of us are broken. Karen and I both married sinners. We are both imperfect. We both need forgiveness, mercy, and grace. This is where the gospel steps in. When we allow the good news of what Christ did for us (despite all our neediness and sinfulness) to transform us, it gives us hope for our marriages.

God is a god of new beginnings. The gospel is good news for our marriages.

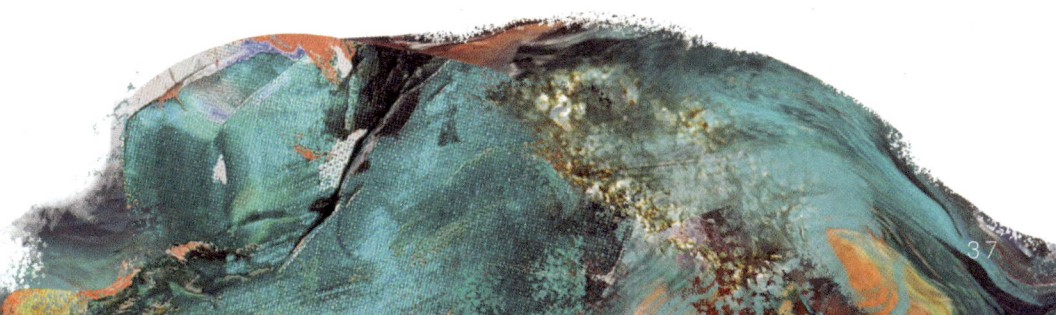

God is a God of *new* BEGINNINGS.

I've always said life is not a snapshot. It's a moving picture. It's not about the bad choices I've made in the past. It's about how, with the Holy Spirit's help, I've corrected those mistakes and how I'm learning from each experience and moving forward. If you've made mistakes in your marriage, don't continue to beat yourself up. We can move forward because of the love of Jesus and what He did for us.

On our wedding day, Karen and I had a choice. We chose to commit—giving ourselves first to God and then each other. It hasn't always been easy. Our faults and shortcomings and failures continue to get on each other's nerves. But we keep going back to those vows—the covenant—we made. That's what it takes for a marriage to endure.

If you're struggling today, let this be a fresh start for you. Your marriage is not beyond hope.

Draw it out:

1. What part of the vows you said on your wedding day do you find easiest to stand by?

2. What kind of marital role models did you have growing up? How did this impact your view of marriage?

3. What do you think a marriage without "exit signs" looks like?

Pray together:

Thank God for the hope He gives us in Jesus for every aspect of our lives—even our marriages. Ask for His help in standing strong in the vows you made to each other on your wedding day. Pray He will use your marriage—no matter where it's at today—to model for others what a lasting marriage looks like. And pray He gets all the glory when you hit that fifty-year mark.

A Weak Marriage Is a Strong Marriage

By David and Meg Robbins

Three times I pleaded with the Lord about this, that it should leave me. But he said to me, "My grace is sufficient for you, for my power is made perfect in weakness." Therefore I will boast all the more gladly of my weaknesses, so that the power of Christ may rest upon me. For the sake of Christ, then, I am content with weaknesses, insults, hardships, persecutions, and calamities. For when I am weak, then I am strong.

2 CORINTHIANS 12:8-10

Early in our marriage, we thought for a couple to be able to influence and help other couples they needed to have everything figured out. Where things not only look like they are going well, but they actually are going well. This, we thought, was the way a Christian marriage should be—a couple who had things in order and surrendered to Jesus in every moment.

But as we think back on what has deeply impacted us and our marriage, it's really had more to do with the not-so-perfect people along the way. Couples who weren't perfect, didn't have everything in order, and may not have surrendered to Jesus in every single moment of their marriage. Yet they were open about their lives and peeled back the curtain to let us see what they were walking through—the good and the bad—and how God was meeting them in those places.

These couples made us realize it's okay to be authentic and be right where we are, weaknesses and all, and to let people see what God is up to in our lives. We realized we didn't have to "arrive" at a certain place in our marriage or spiritual lives in order to trust God or be a marriage on mission.

This rang so true when we moved to New York. We were in a new place asking, "God, how could You use us here?" We didn't have much to offer. We didn't have the education pedigree a lot of people around us had. We didn't come from a cool place. We really felt like we didn't bring much to the table at all.

Until one day, when we were really wrestling with the move, God said to us, "But you have your own journey of brokenness and how I'm working in your life right now. Your marriage is going through things you can crack open and let other people see."

Our response was, "Is that really how You want to do this? You just want us to start being more vulnerable in our own lives and sharing how You're entering into those insecurities, our need for acceptance, and the way we kind of go into control mode with one another?" The answer was . . . yes.
In fact, He wants us to go there with others quicker.

So we started doing all of that in our day-to-day lives. As we did, we realized everyone's normal until you get to know them. And everybody wants someone to get honest, so they can be honest too.

We mistakenly thought our struggles and insecurities were barriers to a marriage that could influence others—whether it was fear or even questions we had about God's goodness in tough times. But time and time again, He has used the hard circumstances we are going through to intertwine our lives with people who are struggling with the same thing.

Second Corinthians says, "My grace is sufficient for you, for my power is made perfect in weakness." This is why a weak marriage is a strong marriage.

No matter what our marriages look like, we still need the

gospel every day. We're not going to come to this place where we've "arrived." We all need to get more comfortable with letting people see how and where we need Jesus on a regular basis. That's what makes Jesus so real to people around us. For some of them, for the first time, they were witnessing how Jesus makes a difference in our lives every day. Not just in the context of eternity, but right now and in every moment.

Dependence on God became one of our goals for our marriage. And if dependence is the goal, then weakness is actually an advantage. Bringing our weakness to the table, living out what Paul lived out in Second Corinthians, boasting in our weakness so that His power could be displayed.

His power made perfect in our weakness.

His power is made

perfect

in our weakness.

Draw it out:

1. Do you think your marriage has an influence on others? Why or why not?

2. On a scale of one to ten—one being not comfortable at all, and ten being very comfortable—how comfortable are you with being honest and vulnerable about the things you're experiencing in marriage?

Pray together:

Thank God for His sufficient grace and that when you are weak, His power is perfect. Ask Him to help you become aware of any barriers you have to being open with others and to help you trust Him in this area. Ask Him to help you be more dependent on Him and to anticipate seeing His perfect power through the weak areas of your marriage.

DABAQ

The perfect word-picture for dabaq is glue. It's a biblical word for sticking together, such as when Ezekiel's tongue literally gets stuck to the roof of his mouth (Ezekiel 3:26) or, in a more poetic connotation, when God commands His people to "hold fast" to Him (Deuteronomy 30:19-20).

Dabaq conveys loyalty and devotion. In the biblical narrative, it is immediately applied to marriage with the man leaving his father and mother and holding fast to his wife. In marriage, a gluing or "dabaq-ing" occurs. Where once two lives unfolded individually, a convergence has taken place. The two do not walk two distinct paths in harmony, but a single path so thoroughly "glued" together that to try and walk separately would ruin them both.

Under every triumph and storm cloud, the dabaq-glue of marriage persists.

Devoted through the Twists and Turns

By Gayla Grace

> *Be devoted to one another in love. Honor one another above yourselves.*
>
> ROMANS 12:10 (NIV)

I could tell something was amiss. My husband, Randy, and I had agreed to meet at a nearby park after work on a beautiful spring afternoon. He was already there when I drove up, tying his sneakers for our walk. As I got out of the car and glanced over, his face told a story I wasn't sure I wanted to know. I walked toward him and asked about his day. My stomach lurched as his words tumbled out.

"I'm no longer an employee. The termination is immediate." Tears glistened in his eyes. "I'll go over in the morning and clean out my office."

I didn't know how to respond. He had relayed his concerns about whether the company was a fit for him. He never suspected an ending like this, however.

Randy and I had moved back to Arkansas for his new job after a ten-year stint in Louisiana. We were thrilled to be back where two of our adult children lived and the hometown where we had dreamed of retiring. We loved everything about this place —the small-town feel, the faith-based community, the beauty of four seasons, and the deep relationships with friends we had raised our kids with. But our dream now felt shattered. *Why, Lord?*

Hard seasons weren't new to us. As a blended family with five kids, our marriage of twenty-seven years has survived ex-spouse drama, defiant stepchildren, a difficult custody battle, the unexpected death of my stepchildren's mom during their teenage years, financial struggles, strained relationships. But this season carried a different kind of hardship. Randy was grieving. He had lost a piece of his identity and was discouraged about the challenge of landing a suitable job at sixty years old. I didn't know how to help.

I turned to God. I cried out, asking for an explanation. But God was silent.

My mind reeled with what the future held. Psalm 34:18 comforted me, "The Lord is near to the brokenhearted and saves the crushed in spirit." But I wanted more. I thought God owed me an answer. We had trusted Him when we relocated for Randy's new job, and it seemed He had let us down. But instead of answering my questions, God pointed me back to my marriage. Did Randy know I would stay by his side, that I would hold fast to the one I loved?

As months of unemployment dragged on with few job possibilities in our town, I watched him dig into His faith to cope. He was hurting. I wanted to do something tangible for him; I wanted to fix it. I'm his designated helpmate, right? But I couldn't change the circumstances. Randy was walking through a valley only he could navigate.

So I began to pray about how to be the wife Randy needed as hard days showed up. I was convinced he needed my opinion with every step. But one day during my morning devotion, Romans 12:10 spoke to me loudly: "Be devoted to one another in love. Honor one another above yourselves" (NIV). I put my Bible down. *What does that really mean?* I prayed. Maybe I was getting it all wrong.

I felt I was devoted to Randy in love. But if I consider that Christ's love is the foundation of how we love others, I always

Honor one another

above yourselves.

ROMANS 12:10 (NIV)

have room for improvement. Christ's love as demonstrated on the cross was selfless, sacrificial, and eternal. Too often, my love for Randy is selfish, looking for something in return. And was I really devoted to him? Was I willing to hold fast to my love for him regardless of the outcome of his job search? Could I accept changes in our financial position without resentment? Or consider relocation . . . again?

What about "honoring one another above yourself"? *The Message* translation says to "practice playing second fiddle." Did I carry a humble heart and consider Randy's needs more important than mine? Did I truly value Randy and express it to him? I needed the Holy Spirit's help on that one.

I continued to pray about how to apply Romans 12:10 in my marriage. Randy needed to see the fruits of the Spirit in my life—patience, kindness, gentleness, etc. (Galatians 5:22-23). And he needed to know I adored him and would stay by his side, regardless of the outcome of his job search. And whatever circumstances showed up in the future.

Thankfully, Randy did land a new job. It wasn't what we expected; he's working 1,900 miles away. But we're learning to enjoy a new season as we explore a different part of the country together. And we continue to work at selfless devotion and honor toward one another as we lean on the Holy Spirit for guidance and understanding with every twist and turn of marriage.

Draw it out:

1. Ask your spouse about one way they sense your devotion—and one potential area of growth.

2. Talk about what "honoring" one another means. Use a commentary or Bible dictionary to get a biblical perspective of the term and how it can be applied.

Pray together:

Ask God how you can be the spouse your partner needs in this season of life. Pray specifically for any struggles they're dealing with right now. Ask God for guidance on how you can better walk with the Holy Spirit as you pursue selflessly loving your spouse.

Draw closer:

Every marriage has its fair share of struggles, but blended families have their own unique set of challenges from the combining of homes, hearts, and histories. Find help for your blended marriage at FamilyLife.com/DrawnTogetherBonus.

This is Your Moment!

By Leslie J. Barner

This is the day that the Lord has made; let us rejoice and be glad in it.

PSALM 118:24

I knew leaving our kids and grandkids to relocate with my job hundreds of miles away would be challenging. This was especially true with my husband, Aubrey, on the heart transplant list, because it also meant leaving his skilled, thoughtful medical team we'd grown to trust and the local support system we had in family and friends. We had to be absolutely certain God was calling us to go.

After seeking Him earnestly for wisdom and direction, His calling was indisputably clear. We were to follow Him to this new place, far away from home. Despite the challenges of taking this leap of faith, we were excited about the move and the house we were building in our new city. We were in this together. Life was good.

Until, suddenly, it wasn't.

About a month into the relocation, a panic attack seized me out of nowhere, plunging me into a deep valley of despair, marked by overwhelming anxiety and depression. I never saw it coming. The next few months were some of the hardest days of my life. I found myself dwelling on the past and worrying about the future. I grieved the comforts of *home* and the close-knit family we left behind. I worried about my husband's impending heart transplant and uncertainty around my new role.

I began to ask God the hard questions like, *Why would You call us so far away from our family and support system at this age and stage of our lives?* I felt trapped and very much alone. In my desperation, I sought the Lord without ceasing. I also reached out to one of the chaplains at work and even tried music therapy. While I was helped in many ways, it was God's grace that held me together when my world was seemingly falling apart.

Then God sent a breakthrough. While preparing to host family for the holidays, I worried about how fast the time with them would pass. I began to grieve their leaving before they even arrived. But in His goodness, God whispered softly to my heart, "Be present. Live in the moment."

I immediately thought about Psalm 16:11: "You make known to me the path of life; in your presence there is fullness of joy; at your right hand are pleasures forevermore." It was an eye opener. While I had been grieving the past and worrying about the future, I was missing out on the blessings of God's provision in the present.

In your presence is *fullness* of *joy...* PSALM 16:11

Being present during the holidays made all the difference, and I experienced so much peace and joy. But God continued to speak to my heart about *presence*, until finally, I understood He was also calling me to be present in my marriage. I thought about how alone Aubrey must have felt during all those months I struggled with transition in isolation. I was saddened that during that time I lost sight of what was true. I had forgotten Aubrey was *with* me and *for* me all along. For months, I didn't even truly see him.

Additionally, I was reminded life is but "a mist that appears for a little time and then vanishes" (James 4:14). This truth helped me see that by not being present, I was missing out on precious time with "him whom my soul loves" (Solomon 3:4).

I shifted from struggling in isolation, to moving toward Aubrey. I began to see him, and to allow him to see me. I shared my challenges and my pain with him in real time; and in turn, made sure he also felt heard. And I began to find joy in spending quality time together, talking, laughing, exploring our new city, and creatively making our new house a home.

I was finally able to find—and give—the love, support, and encouragement we both needed during this tough transition. Being present was a game changer not only for improving my spiritual, mental, and emotional health, but also for the health of our marriage as we navigated our new life challenges and joys *together*.

Draw it out:

1. Share with each other what being present in marriage looks like to you.

2. Talk about the difference it would make in your relationship . if you were both present in your marriage. Then share honestly with each other what, if anything, has kept you from being present.

3. Commit to each other one long-term change you could make today to help your spouse feel seen, heard, and valued.

Pray together:

Thank God for giving you the gift of His presence, and for all that can be found in Him (joy, peace, strength, comfort, pleasures). Ask Him to help you both to be present in your marriage, and that in doing so, you will come to intimately know, truly connect, and deeply love each other today and every day, as you navigate life together.

Grieving In Green Pastures

By Daniel and Christina Im

> *The Lord is my shepherd; I shall not want.*
> *He makes me lie down in green pastures.*
> *He leads me beside still waters.*

PSALM 23:1-2

If life is like a journey, grief can be a landslide that irrevocably alters your path. It can leave you radically disoriented, severely injured, and seemingly alone. Which is a real problem. Especially if you're married and intended to journey through life with your spouse.

When Daniel's father died just sixteen months after his cancer diagnosis, each of us experienced heart-shattering grief. But we experienced it in such different ways it was hard to feel like we were still even on the same path.

Daniel is an expert compartmentalizer and naturally took on a helper role for his newly widowed mom. While I (Christina) understood and agreed his mom needed help from her son during this difficult time, I was experiencing my own grief and often felt alone. I wanted to grieve alongside my husband, not separate from him. We found our way back to each other, but, like so many things in marriage, the path turned out to be different than we expected.

If it hasn't already, grief will certainly make its mark on your marriage: maybe in bereavement, job loss, unfulfilled dreams, betrayal, mental illness, or any other manner of loss. How do you weather these life events with one-flesh intimacy when it feels like the ground might swallow you at any moment?

We found two principles that helped us.

Space. Space sounds bad, if grief is like meandering through a treacherous forest, with all manner of danger lurking behind every tree. However, what if Jesus—our Good Shepherd—can transform even the path of grief into a wide, green space? What if He can comfort one of you with a cool drink from a gentle stream, while the other draws comfort from lying in the soft grass?

We've found there's no real roadmap, no formula you can both follow at the same pace to arrive at the finish line at the end of grief. (And some grief never ends. It just changes.) We each needed space to process grief in our own ways. Grief will always be a little lonely, because no one experiences your losses exactly as you do. Jesus is the only One who ever understands every tear, fear, sigh, or cry of anguish.

But that doesn't mean you and your spouse can't still journey together, even if you're experiencing grief in different ways. One of the best things you can do is talk about it. So—

Share. Acknowledge you're grieving differently, and seek to understand each other without trying to "fix" your spouse. Allow each other to voice tough questions, and don't minimize whatever they're feeling. Jesus' green pastures hold enough breadth for you both.

Regular check-ins using a couple of key phrases were our saving grace when we were in a season of deep grief: "I feel" and "I need." For instance, when Daniel was spending time away helping his mom adjust to her new life, I told him, "Honey, I feel really lonely with you away so much right now, even though I totally agree it's important. I need time to connect. When you get back, can we go on a date?"

Sharing honestly about our feelings and needs not only helped us to process our grief for our self-understanding, but also really helped cultivate togetherness in our marriage. In a season that could honestly have led to intense loneliness, misunderstandings, and drifting impossibly far apart from each other, we grew in understanding, compassion, and intimacy with and for each other.

Life's journey inevitably brings grief. But you don't need undue fear that these seasons will drive an irreparable wedge in your marriage. Our Good Shepherd Jesus intimately knows every grief and can lead you both with great gentleness and care. There is enough space, in Him, for you both to heal and regain strength to continue your journey—together.

The Lord is my *shepherd;*

I shall not want.

He makes me lie down in green pastures.

He leads me

beside *still* waters.

PSALM 23:1–2

Draw it out:

1. Have you and your spouse encountered a season of grief as a couple? Do you feel you were drawn closer together? Why or why not?

2. How might these two principles of *space* and *sharing* help you weather seasons of grief? Might they even help for other seasons?

3. Take a few moments to check in today, using "I feel" and "I need" statements.

Pray together:

Thank God for being such a compassionate, tender, and kind God. Acknowledge that He is a Good Shepherd who can be trusted to lead you through any season and bring you safely home. Spend some time using the "I feel" and "I need" statements with God, knowing He longs to comfort and encourage you.

Marriage Isn't Just Peaceful Coexistence

By Dennis and Barbara Rainey

How good and pleasant it is when God's people live together in unity!

PSALM 133:1 (NIV)

Dennis and I (Barbara) went on vacation one summer and stayed at this remote, cute little farmhouse. It should have been the perfect place to connect. The only problem was there was absolutely nothing to do around there.

As I wandered around the house, I noticed a shelf in one of the rooms with all kinds of books on it. After looking through the selection for a few minutes, I found one I wanted to read. I brought it downstairs and sat down with this massive, 800-page book. Dennis knew if I started reading it, I would get so engrossed he wouldn't see me for the next twenty-four hours. He looked at me and said, "You're not going to start reading *that* are you?"

"Well, yeah. I am," I told him.

I would have been fine spending the weekend curled up reading by myself, but that wouldn't have been an enjoyable vacation for him. More importantly, it wouldn't have done anything to help us reconnect with each other, which was the whole point of the trip. But instead of fighting me about it, he said, "Well, let's just read it together then."

Dennis proceeded to read a chapter, and then I read a chapter. We went back and forth and read the entire book together over the course of that week. It was great. We discovered this fun new experience that we'd never done before. Since then, we've occasionally found a book and read it aloud together.

I (Dennis) think some marriages that look successful may conceal two people doing their own thing, like Barbara and I might have wanted to do in that farmhouse: peacefully coexisting. Roommates. Those relationships sometimes unravel because they haven't been growing together as a couple.

I know when Barbara and I first married, we had some big ideals about what a Christian marriage was supposed to look like. Things like having time in the Bible together, sitting down for breakfast and sharing from the Scripture, and talking about what we wrote in our journals at the end of the day. But I can say, after more than five decades of marriage, it has not turned out that way.

Marriage is a union between two selfish and sinful human beings. Barbara and I don't always want to do things together—or even spend our own vacation the same way. We don't always want to compromise. We've had to work for every inch of connection in our marriage, and it hasn't always been easy. Sometimes, the most important work happens in those unexpected little moments where we choose to do life together rather than apart.

Christian marriage should have, as its unmistakable characteristic, not just two people who share journal entries, but two people willing to give up their lives for the other (check out Phillipians 2:1-11). To do what is best for your spouse—to grow closer to your spouse—even when you just don't want to. In those moments when it was easier to do nothing or to simply go our separate ways, Barbara and I had to press in and make little sacrifices to develop our friendship as a couple. She could have refused my offer to read that massive book with her and told me she preferred to read alone. I could have chosen to entertain myself by going fishing. But in marriage, we must constantly choose to make sacrifices in order to grow closer together.

I'll give you another example. Barbara likes gardening. Personally, I believe that if God intended flowers to grow in our yard, he'd have put them there in the first place. But Barbara likes to subdue the earth and rule over it (Genesis 1:28). That means I have a choice. I could let her do it alone, or I could find a way to join her. So, guess what I've done over the past fifty years? I've learned how to garden.

And you know what? I've realized that it is really quite fascinating. Through it, I've gained a fresh appreciation for one of the most fantastic declarations of the image of God anywhere on this planet: flowers. Not to mention Barbara beaming with a smile because of what we'd accomplished together. Gardening not only feeds my relationship with God, but it's also helping me appreciate another one of His amazing creations—my wife.

Draw it out:

1. Achieving oneness always involves some level of sacrifice. What is one thing you think stands in the way of a stronger friendship with your spouse?

2. What is one activity your spouse enjoys that you could choose to participate in?

3. What is one activity you love that you could invite your spouse to participate in?

Pray together:

Thank God for the unique way He made your spouse, including the things they enjoy doing that you might not. Ask Him to help you see the beauty in His creation and His wisdom in putting the two of you together. Ask God to open your eyes to new ways of connecting with your spouse and developing your friendship.

Marriage Is Fun, Too

By Jackie and Stephana Bledsoe

Enjoy life with the wife whom you love...

ECCLESIASTES 9:9

We remember it like it was yesterday. We had committed to having weekly dates by any means necessary, so we decided to have an impromptu lunch date and trip to the gym together. But this date didn't end as expected.

We made a quick run to Sam's Club to pick up a few things while we were in the area. But as we walked in, we had some misunderstandings over (of all the things to argue about...) Stephana's purse. As she was trying to fit her belongings into it, I (Jackie) tried to give her all the ways she could make it work. Honestly, we probably spent more time in the parking lot arguing back and forth over her purse than we did in the store.

Then on the drive home we *continued* to rehash the conversation we had in the parking lot of Sam's Club, both of us sharing "our version" of what happened. But a minute or so in, we lost it. We both completely exploded—in laughter! We cracked up as we realized how silly the entire argument really was. We laughed the rest of the way home. I'm sure the people driving next to us thought we were crazy. What could have turned into a heated argument and hours (or even days) of the silent treatment, turned into a fun, funny, and memorable experience together.

It's times like these that remind us how important it is to have fun together. We hear and read so much about marriage being hard. And it is. But hearing, "marriage is hard" over and over again can make you forget marriage is fun, too.

The difference is, it's naturally hard for two biologically different people, with different backgrounds, different experiences, and different expectations of marriage to come together in holy matrimony. But having fun in marriage takes intentionality.

It's said, "couples who pray together, stay together." You could say the same about fun in marriage: "Couples who have fun together, become one together." Solomon teaches us this in Ecclesiastes and Proverbs as he says, "Enjoy life with the wife whom you love," (Ecclesiastes 9:9) and "A joyful heart is good medicine" (Proverbs 17:22).

We've experienced some of the bonuses, too.

- Building positive memories together.
- Strengthening your friendship.
- Providing opportunities to laugh.
- Bonding and reconnecting, especially after an argument or challenge.
- Improving your communication.
- Building trust.
- Encouraging sexual intimacy.

As we mentioned earlier, the "marriage is hard" part comes naturally. The "marriage is fun" part does not. And if you're like us, one spouse's definition of fun may not be the other spouse's definition. But even with our differences, we've been able to create simple, shared experiences we both enjoy.

- Walks around the neighborhood.
- Working out at the gym together.
- Just being together to watch our boys' baseball games.
- Even finding a good spot to sit beside each other to people watch.

We try to plan regular date nights, but we've learned the best way to have a fun date night is to make sure we are connecting throughout the week leading up to it. So we've committed to talking everyday—at least fifteen minutes of conversation—with just us and no distractions. As we began to consistently have those small interactions through talking everyday and shared experiences through weekly dates, we began to discover more about each other. We learned the definition of fun for both of us.

You've heard, "Find a job you enjoy, and you'll never 'work' a day in your life." The same can be applied to your marriage. Find ways to have fun in your marriage, and marriage might just feel less hard.

A *joyful heart* IS GOOD MEDICINE.

PROVERBS 17:22

Draw it out:

1. What are some things you do to have fun in your marriage?

2. Do you see weekly dates as a doable way to connect? If so, grab your calendars. If not, what's another way to more regularly inject some fun into your moments together?

3. Create a shared list of fun things to do you haven't done yet. How can you get intentional about making them a reality?

Pray together:

Thank God for creating you both in His image, so you can have fun and laugh and experience joy. Thank Him for marriage so you have someone to share the fun. Ask Him to help you intentionally choose to have more fun in your marriage and to fill your hearts with happiness day after day.

Sticky Notes of Faith

By Ashford Sonii

> *Death and life are in the power of the tongue,*
> *and those who love it will eat its fruits.*

PROVERBS 18:21

The thought of losing our girls chased us for three months.

Through emergency c-section at 30 weeks of pregnancy, Olivia and I became parents to Ivey and Oakley, born at one pound, eleven ounces and three pounds, four ounces. As doctors rushed our girls to the Neonatal Intensive Care Unit (NICU), we had no idea how hard the next season would hit us.

It seemed every test and procedure landed on their charts: heart evaluations, belly scans, intubation and extubation, multiple PIC lines, UV lights for bilirubin, electrolyte fluids. Our stress levels were sky high and anxiety ran wild.

After a week went by, Liv said, "I feel everyone but me is helping our girls, and I'm their mom!" Those words made me feel I was failing all three of my girls. I couldn't help our daughters get better. I couldn't comfort my wife enough to ease her mind. I thought, *What good am I as a husband and new father?*

One morning, God laid Proverbs 18:21 on my mind, "Death and life are in the power of the tongue, and those who love it will eat its fruits."

The following day, I grabbed sticky notes and markers before heading to the hospital. When we arrived at the NICU, I sat close to Olivia and gently said, "God reminded me we actually have power. For every negative NICU report, we'll pronounce good things over Ivey and Oakley. We can jot statements on the sticky notes and place them on their wall each time. Let's stand on God's Word and speak over our girls' lives."

Seemingly uninterested, Olivia placed the sticky notes to the side and declined the idea to write anything down. I was devastated. I was trying to help by reminding her of our God-given spiritual authority. It seemed she was being oppositional.

I ignorantly thought, *Aren't we on the same team of faith? Why are you acting this way?* I had the urge to scrap the idea and just focus on me. Processing my own emotions was hard enough. Instead, I prayed. "God, I need your help. I feel like I'm moving according to Your plan, but please give me strength or graciously correct me if I'm wrong."

God affirmed in my heart that I was heading in His direction but that I also needed to understand Olivia's perspective. She was a first time mom who just had twins at thirty weeks through emergency c-section—after the roller coaster of harsh preeclampsia symptoms. I had to consider how I'd feel seeing our twins in the NICU after trying my best to carry them.

I was emotionally oblivious. But God designed me to love Olivia like Jesus loves the church: passionately, patiently and perseveringly. His way was the answer.

I continued pursuing Olivia and held on to the sticky-notes idea. I expressed love and curiosity for her well-being, asking questions like: "How do you feel that went?" "Can I tell you how I'm feeling and you go next?" I hadn't verbalized my emotions to her. I assumed she knew I was hurting, too. When we both were fatigued or annoyed, I just hugged her (despite my feelings), placing my hand on her head, praying silently for her mind. She started doing the same for me.

Later, she told me how she felt when I shared the sticky notes with her. She said, "I feel responsible for the girls being in the NICU. Are the girls going to make it?" I affirmed the situation was not her fault at all. "I don't know the future, but I trust the One who holds it," I said. She confessed she couldn't see past our girls' current condition to exercise faith in God's promises. I was humbled when she said, "I was asking God if I could just have faith like yours."

Over the following weeks, we shared more about how we were feeling, and I continued posting sticky notes on the walls.

- Ivey and Oakley have great lungs!
- Ivey is a super pooper!
- Ivey and Oakley are coming home with mom and dad.

The sticky notes I wrote began coming true. That's when Olivia decided to join. Three months later, the notes formed art as our twins graduated from the NICU with good health and every sticky-note prayer answered.

When we experience hard circumstances, the stress can threaten to pull us apart. In the middle of a crisis, it'd just be easier to take care of yourself, right?

Challenges can seem too difficult to navigate together, but sticking with your spouse both keeps your vows and honors God. You receive strength to achieve and maintain oneness. When struggling to stay close to your spouse during a hard time, taking your pain to God is a great place to start.

Almost losing our girls stretched the limits of our relationship. We didn't get everything right. But, today, as we rock our little toddlers to sleep, I'm thankful God led me to cling to my spouse when the waves got rough. During a storm, surrendering our choices to Jesus will always bring the best outcome for our marriages and our faith.

Draw it out:

1. What hard situation is your marriage facing? How can you cling to your spouse through this time?

2. The next time life threatens the oneness between you and your spouse—it might be today—try writing some "sticky notes of faith" to speak life into your marriage. Here are some ideas:

- We are one flesh (Matthew 19:4-6).

- We are stronger together!

- We will not let the Enemy come between us (Ephesians 4:27).

Pray together:

Thank God that He never pulls away from us when life is challenging. Ask for His help when the urge arises to walk away from your spouse or your marriage when things feel tough. Pray for the strength and wisdom to speak life into your marriage, trusting God's hand is over you both.

The In-between

By Carlos Santiago

*For the mountains may depart and the hills be removed,
but my steadfast love shall not depart from you, and
my covenant of peace shall not be removed," says the
LORD, who has compassion on you.*

ISAIAH 54:10

We're a high-maintenance couple. If my wife and I go a day without talking over a cup of coffee or taking a walk around the neighborhood, we feel it. Without spending intentional, quality time with each other, we quickly get out of sync. Our patience wears thin, our tones get harsh, and bickering over small things increases.

We're not alone. The drift from order to chaos is the natural way of the universe. (Yes, the second law of thermodynamics applies to relationships, too.) Over time, the chaos in my relationship will increase. I *will* grow apart from my spouse, I *will* lose the ability to talk to my children, my faith *will* fade, and the family harmony we once had *will* be lost. *Unless* I actively and intentionally fight against the drift.

The word translated as "hold fast" in Genesis 2:24 is "dabaq." It means to cleave, to cling or adhere, to catch by pursuit, to follow hard after, be joined (together), overtake, to pursue hard. You must pursue each other hard and "hold on tight" because there will be forces trying to tear your marriage apart from the moment you say, "I do."

But my

steadfast love

shall not depart

from you . . .

ISAIAH 54:10

Some forces feel big and obvious to me, like a sudden sickness, job loss, parenting a special-needs child, or night school. Other forces might be more subtle, like spending too much time scrolling a phone, binge-watching shows, or playing video games. They seem harmless, maybe even enjoyable, but over time, they have a similar effect. Like my wife and I, maybe one day you'll notice you've drifted so far away from your spouse you don't know if you have the strength to make it back. Whether the distance comes all at once or develops slowly over the years, our instinct is to do nothing. But God calls us to "dabaq"—to hold on tight and not allow ourselves to drift apart, to take the walks and talk over the lattes. And when we notice there is distance, to pursue each other ... hard. But how?

Early in our marriage, when I felt distant from my wife, I'd try to reconnect with a date night or vacation. The greater the distance I felt, the more elaborate my plans would get. The problem was that getting my grand ideas out of my head became a challenge. Plans for this weekend would drift to the next. Next weekend became next month. Next month became next year. All the while, the distance between us continued to grow. While date nights and vacations should be a regular part of your marriage's rhythm, when we expect them to repair the distance developed over the course of months or even years, we're setting ourselves up for disappointment.

Most of us want to have a good (or better) relationship with our spouse. I know my wife and I do. But sometimes we can't figure out how, or we make excuses and rely on quality time over quantity. But this never really gets us where we want to go. My wife and I don't just need the mountaintop experiences; we need the in-between, too. We need both quantity and quality. We need to find small ways to fight the drift and reconnect. It might be something as simple as greeting each other with a hug at the end of each workday, sending a text, or sharing a cup of chamomile tea after the kids have been put to bed, depending on your season of life. But the most important thing is consistency. An established foundation of reliable connections takes the pressure off date nights. Instead of looking to them to fix problems, they can simply be times of celebration.

My wife and I haven't always done this well. There have been times we've let busyness and general complacency create distance. We've allowed ourselves to get caught up in going through the motions of life, and we've neglected each other. But because of the little habits of connection we developed over the years, it usually doesn't take long before we notice the drift and start correcting our course back toward each other. Sure, we still love date nights and vacations, but we no longer live for the peak moments. The in-betweens are just as sweet.

Draw it out:

1. What are the biggest forces pulling at your marriage? What are the less obvious ones that impact the day-to-day connection?

2. What little things mean the most to you? (Compliments, holding hands, acts of service, etc.)

3. Recall a "little thing" your spouse did that helped you feel close.

Pray together:

Ask God to help you know which forces pulling you from your spouse can be controlled— and which can't. Ask Him to show you ways you can "hold fast" to your spouse.

I'm for You

By Trent Griffith

Therefore shall a man leave his father and his mother, and shall cleave unto his wife: and they shall be one flesh.

GENESIS 2:24 (KJV)

The woman I married didn't have cancer. But the woman I found myself married to fifteen years later did.

It was already the most stressful season of our lives. We were in the second year of planting a new church, while Andrea was homeschooling our four kids ages thirteen, twelve, nine, and six. That's when we received the phone call that would change our lives. The voice on the other end of the call was from an oncologist ready to schedule treatment for cancer we didn't yet know was threatening Andrea's life.

I remember selfishly thinking, "God, we're too busy for this. Don't You see how we're serving You? I need a healthy wife. I didn't sign up for this."

But God reminded me of the part of our wedding vows most of us gloss over at the altar: "For better or *worse*. In *sickness* and in health. 'Till *death* do us part." This was the worst, the sickness, and it could lead to death. At that moment, I had a choice to make. Would I cleave to my wife as I had promised, or would I drift away from my God-given assignment to carry my wife and family through the worst? I certainly didn't do it perfectly or even happily at times, but God made it clear to me, "You did sign up for this."

In that season, holding fast meant moving toward my wife as her greatest ally in her most difficult battle. It meant being with her through every doctor's appointment, surgery, and treatment. It meant becoming a homeschooling dad. It meant spending our savings on medical expenses when I would rather have spent it on myself. It meant "dabaq."

In the King James Version of the Bible, the Hebrew word "dabaq" is translated into the English word "cleave." It's an interesting word. It actually has two opposite meanings. The first definition of "cleave" is "to make one into two." If you are preparing a meal and you need to make one big chunk of meat into two, your utensil of choice will likely be a "cleaver." The second definition is "to make two into one." That's the biblical use of the word cleave. Each spouse in marriage is a cleaver, waking up each day in the pursuit of oneness no matter what the unforeseen challenges.

Choosing to draw close when your spouse is in pain may be the greatest demonstration of what it means to cleave. It's a lot easier to "cleave" to a spouse who is healthy, happy, and hopeful. But when the aging process, financial pressures, and occupational responsibilities affect your spouse negatively, it can make cleaving as difficult as snuggling with a porcupine.

I'm happy to report Andrea has been cancer-free for over a decade now. Yet, my sciatica—which I also didn't have yet on our wedding day—is still a pain for both of us. The literal pain in my posterior can make me a pain in Andrea's. But I'm grateful she keeps cleaving to this porcupine at the risk of getting pricked by my grumpiness.

You already know difficulties are unavoidable in a fallen world. Believe it or not, couples who drift apart and couples who remain together for a lifetime essentially face the same set of difficulties. The only difference is whether we choose to cleave to one another, or if we'll allow the pain to drive a wedge between us.

I love that throughout the Bible, God promises His presence in our pain: "The Lord himself goes before you and will be with you; he will never leave you nor forsake you. Do not be afraid; do not be discouraged" (Deuteronomy 31:8, NIV). I take so much comfort in knowing God is with me and for me even when life is hard. The unexpected difficulties can be a great gift, because it moves me into a deeper and more intimate relationship with our Lord.

Similarly, being present in Andrea's pain brought intimacy we would not have otherwise experienced. I suddenly held opportunities to communicate being "for" her by choosing to be present physically, emotionally, and spiritually. It's a kind of presence oncologists, financial advisors, or therapists can't provide. The ministry of presence can be as simple as showing up in the same room or it can be as intimate as a warm embrace during lovemaking in a season of suffering.

While God's presence is available for Andrea in a way I can never be, I can show presence, kindness, and encouragement while my spouse is waiting for the physical presence of her Savior.

Draw it out:

1. Reflect on your wedding vows. Which of your unexpected difficulties falls into the categories of *worse*, *poorer*, and *sickness*?

2. How have you seen these things drive you together or pull you apart?

3. Ask your spouse, "What can I do or say this week to communicate I am for you?"

Pray together:

Thank God that He is with you and for you. Thank Him for the gift of your spouse and ask for His help in fully cleaving to them during whatever season your marriage is in or will ultimately go through. Pray for Him to show you ways to tangibly communicate, "I am for you."

1-4-3

By Lisa Lakey

> *So now faith, hope, and love abide, these three; but the greatest of these is love.*
>
> 1 CORINTHIANS 13:13

Back when my now-husband and I were dating, shooting a quick text was a nonexistent feature of our cellular communication (I know, this dates us a bit). Sure, we could text … but quickly? Not so much. For those of you who didn't have the privilege of playing snake on an old Nokia, let me explain.

Each letter from two to nine had a series of three to four letters each. To simply type the letter "I," I had to punch the number four button three times. To spell out the short text I sent him the most often? Twenty-three key presses including spaces. It felt like a lot for three little words, but at the time, there wasn't anything I'd rather do than type, *I love you.* But if I needed to shoot him a quick reminder on the fly? I'd send a quick "1-4-3," the number of letters in each word of my favorite phrase.

Cheesy, right? Early love typically is with all its dream-filled talks, lingering kisses, and heart eyes, even if it was technologically archaic. But one thing technology won't change is the need to hear "I love you" on the regular. It's amazing what that simple phrase can convey depending on the context of what's going on in your marriage.

Early in the relationship, it's a promise. *I love you and want to spend the rest of my life with you. I'm so lucky to have you.* When trials come in a marriage, it's a beacon of light. *This is hard. But I love you, and we'll get through this together. We're still a team.* When (not if) marriage is extra tough, it's another inch when we're at the end of our rope. *I love you. Hold on a little longer. I'm still rooting for us.* And when you're on the other side of those struggles, it's a reaffirmation of what you might have forgotten. *I love you, and I'm glad you're in this with me. Together, we can tackle anything.*

Your spouse will never stop needing to hear it, because every time you do, you're saying, "I choose you." *I choose to spend the rest of my life with you, I choose to get through the trials with you, and I will choose to hold on a little longer, even when the weight of life threatens to pull us apart.* Why? Because 1 Corinthians 13:7-8 reminds us: "Love bears all things, believes all things, hopes all things, endures all things. Love never ends."

But the
GREATEST
of these is

1 CORINTHIANS 13:13

But that doesn't always feel true, does it? That's because love is a choice more than a feeling that ebbs and flows with circumstance. It's a constant choosing, really. It was a choice when, as a young dating couple, we wrapped our arms around each other after our first fight. We both still felt the sting of an argument not easily resolved, but we chose to move toward each other anyway.

Love was a choice after the birth of our first child, when we discovered balancing marriage and parenthood was way harder than we had imagined. Priorities were skewed, sleep was in short supply, and hateful words were spewed as tears were shed. But then a hand reached out to grip mine, fingers lacing together in a silent promise—choosing to hold on even when we weren't sure we wanted to. A whispered "I love you" reminded us both we could bear, believe, hope, and endure a little longer. So we did. And it's been a choice every day since.

Will it be hard sometimes? Absolutely. But keep choosing anyway. That's what creates a deeper, more vulnerable, more meaningful love. You've been given all you need to love your spouse in the good times, in the hard times, in the "I don't want to do this anymore" times. Because when you both find yourselves at the end of your rope? It's God's love that keeps you holding on. First John 4: reminds us: "God is love, and whoever abides in love abides in God, and God abides in him. . . . We love because he first loved us."

So never stop saying "I love you." Or if you're really feeling nostalgic, send 'em a quick 1-4-3.

Draw it out:

1. Is saying "I love you" a regular part of your daily rhythm as a couple? If not, ask yourself why that is.

2. Do you remember the first time each of you said, "I love you"? If you can, reflect with each other on that moment and what led you to say those three little words.

3. Today, in what ways do you see love as more of a choice than a feeling?

Pray together:

Start by thanking God for His unending love for you—that He chooses to love you despite your rebellion, your selfishness, and those other secret parts of you that only He can see. Pray that this type of love would flow through your relationship with Him and into your marriage. Ask for His help in continually choosing to love your spouse through the good, okay, and downright hard times you and your spouse will inevitably go through.

AGAPE

The ancient Greeks were more specific with the word "love" than we are, employing four different words. The highest form is agape love: a self-denying love aiming to benefit someone else. It is a love that bleeds. Agape love isn't based on emotion, but decision. It is shown by action. God decided to agape love us and it cost Him greatly (John 3:16). It is a pure, unconditional love.

Following Jesus, we extend agape love, to our spouse in marriage. If marriage wanes into any lesser love, that marriage is crippled. If you wait for your spouse to deserve your self-denying love, it is not agape love. This, of course, contradicts human nature. Agape love, therefore, requires a new self which only Jesus can bring. This is a Christian's love, which we showcase to the world in marriage.

Squishy Definitions of Love

By Crawford Loritts

Let no one seek his own good, but the good of his neighbor.

1 CORINTHIANS 10:24

The day I met Karen, I had sworn off dating. My high-school sweetheart had just broken up with me a few weeks before, and I was hurting. I remember praying that day and saying, "I'm not going to date anybody this semester. It's just You and me, Jesus." But then I walked across campus, opened a door, and there she was. Suddenly, I was healed.

Karen, of course, remembers our first meeting a bit differently. She'll tell you she was "unimpressed" when she first met me. I'm not so sure about that, but either way, we've been together for more than fifty years now.

As you probably already know, from the moment you meet to long after you say "I do," you and your spouse are going to have differences. Differences in your likes and dislikes, in how you perceive an argument, even in how you remember things.

There's a tendency to assume that "oneness" in marriage means "sameness." And that's just not true. Karen is not identical to me, doesn't always have the same feelings and ideas as me. She doesn't even feel loved in the same way I do.

For example, I often bring my wife flowers. I want her to know I love and appreciate her. But it isn't the flowers that make her feel loved and appreciated. Instead, she feels most loved when I take care of the things she hates doing most: taking out the trash and cleaning the floors. So I made those my regular chores around the house. I don't do these because I enjoy them, but because I love my wife.

There's a lot of squishy definitions about love, but love is beyond just the feeling. In fact, there's no such thing as true love without some sort of sacrifice. As Paul wrote in 1 Corinthians, "Let no one seek his own good, but the good of his neighbor" (verse 10:24). And it's the kind of love described all over 1 Corinthians 13: "Love is patient and kind … does not envy or boast … is not arrogant or rude. It does not insist on its own way..." (verses 4-5).

True love doesn't always mean compromise or win-win situations. Exhibiting true love for my wife means I will disadvantage myself for the comfort and benefit of Karen. Even if that means scrubbing floors.

love...
...DOES NOT
INSIST
ON IT'S
own way...
1 CORINTHIANS 10:24

I once heard someone say that when you say your vows, you're talking about a present love—based on how you feel about your new spouse in that moment. But real love is a future love. We're seeing that now in friends who have been married for decades and are now caregivers to their husbands or wives. And you see that "future love" now being manifested.

As you get older and are married longer, there are going to be a lot of things you don't like about one another, and those small differences will lead to arguments. Then there are things you don't expect—like sicknesses that come along—and you might even think you didn't sign up for this. But that's when real love comes in. That true love that denies self (your preferences, desires, and even what annoys you) and becomes a sacrificial offering to do what is best for the one you love.

Make no mistake: Love is not denial. Love does not deny the fact that your spouse gets on your everlasting nerves every once in a while. Karen and I still drive each other crazy at times. When we got married, she had no choice but to marry a sinner. As sweet as she is, she's a sinner too. And as a sinner myself, loving another sinner is not easy.

None of this feels natural, right? We won't love our spouses perfectly, I certainly haven't over the last fifty years. But we have help. First John 4:7 tells us "love is from God." So how do we practically do this in our marriages?

First, own your stuff. If I act in an unloving way toward Karen, even if I think I'm triggered by something she did, I have to own it. I need to acknowledge to God (and my wife) that my attitude was wrong.

Then I need to ask God to show me a better way. A better way to love my wife as the gift He's given me. Because His ways are always better than my own.

Draw it out:

1. Take an honest and humble assessment. How well do you do with valuing your spouse above yourself?

2. Share some examples of when you feel your spouse valued you above themselves?

3. Write 1 Corinthians 10:24 in your journal or somewhere you'll see it often and read it aloud to yourself at the start of each day for a week.

Pray together:

Thank God for the unending source of love He gives you through your relationship with Him. Acknowledge any ways you may have been selfish in your marriage. Ask for God to help you discover ways to better love your spouse in the days ahead.

Love Drugs

By Derwin and Vicki Gray

> *But God has so composed the body, giving greater honor to the part that lacked it, that there may be no division in the body, but that the members may have the same care for one another.*

1 CORINTHIANS 12:24-25

When we first met, I (Derwin) was like, "Man, I love how she just steps in and takes charge. She'll get things done. She's awesome."

When you fall in love, get married, and you both say, "I do," you're wide open. Everything is great! The grass is greener, the sky is bluer, food tastes better, even their sweat is a sweet aroma! It's like you're on this super high, almost like you are on love drugs.

Seriously. Scientifically, there's something that happens to make you feel this way. God designed us in a way that when we fall in love, our brains are flooded with dopamine and serotonin. So we walk around, or float around, basically high from these love drugs. You don't see anything wrong with your spouse.

This lasts for about four years. Then, around the four-and-a-half year mark, things start to calm down. You come down from your love-drug high and you have to learn to live in marriage . . . sober. Actually, this is when you have to learn how to rely on Christ and walk in the power of the Spirit to love your spouse the way God wants you to. This is when things get real in marriage. Going into year five, I was like, "Man, she's bossy. She's telling me what to do. And I'm a grown man!" The high from those love drugs had gone away. Real love and life were setting in.

Let me give you another example. I'm a visionary. I constantly come up with these ideas. I would come to Vicki, saying something like, "Babe, I got an idea. It's the greatest idea in the world!" And I would cast vision. I mean, I'd be really passionate about my vision while sharing it with her. I'd be sweating, and spit would be coming out my mouth. After sharing, I'd say, "This is awesome. What do you think?"

Of course, I'd expect my passion and excitement to be reflected in her response. Instead, her response would be along the lines of, "Well, how are we going to do it?"

Immediately, I would say, "There you go. Oh, look at the dream killer in full effect. A brother can't even dream for a minute before you start tearing it up."

My response was not because of her, but because of my own insecurity. It took going through a session at FamilyLife's Weekend to Remember marriage getaway for us to realize what was happening. Over the weekend, we learned about each other's personality styles, which are completely different. I (Vicki) learned the way God wired Derwin was to see far ahead, to be a visionary, to ideate and come up with ideas and talk philosophically. It drove me crazy.

At the same time, I (Derwin) thought she was trying to irritate me and trying to kill my dreams. We'd go back and forth, with Vicki responding, "You're trying to kill me. Because who is going to do all this work?" The love-drug high had clearly worn off, and now we both thought we were intentionally trying to irritate and kill each other.

But then I (Vicki) came to a realization and said, "Wait, God, You made him that way? He's not just doing that to irritate me, right?"

Once we recognized this, we really learned how to complete one another instead of competing with one another. The way this looks in our marriage today is when I'm stuck in the details and the practicality of life, I'll say, "Hey, what do you see? How do you think this could go?" Or he'll come to me and say, "Can this even work?"

We've learned to recognize and appreciate that we have these differences, which we probably didn't even really notice in those love-drug years of our marriage. Now, as we look back at the sovereign hand of God, we realize our differences are often what the other lacks. But together, it makes us a team that does everything from plant churches to parent our kids. Two individuals who now see each other complementing one another, not competing with one another. All done without depending on feelings induced by love drugs.

Draw it out:

1. List and discuss some ways you are different from one another.

2. Discuss how your specific differences complement one another.

3. What are some ways you can function better as a team and not compete with each other?

Pray together:

Thank God for bringing you together as two unique people. Thank Him for wiring you in a way that you can experience the "high" of being in love and being filled with His love. When your differences clash, ask God to gently remind you both that God created each of you how you are, and, when you come together in His name, He can make something beautiful from your differences.

Cheering You On

By Aaron and Jamie Ivey

> *Beloved, if God so loved us, we also ought to love one another. No one has ever seen God; if we love one another, God abides in us and his love is perfected in us.*

1 JOHN 4:11-12

Early on in our marriage, I (Aaron) started to notice that between work, church, and other social circles, somebody was always going to notice good things about Jamie. And frankly, I was falling down on the job.

As her husband, I wanted, needed, to be cheering for her the most. I want Jamie to feel that no one speaks worth and value to her like I do. I was being out-cheered.

Speaking for the two of us, we've found we have to continually go back to the Author of love. God's love for us is sacrificial, unconditional, and never-ending. It's more than affection, which is constantly changing. As image-bearers, we were designed for the same kind of love. If I love you because you love me, that won't stand up against the challenges of life. Our love needs to run deeper than a transactional perspective, shifting from a mindset of "What can you do for me?" to "How do I continue to love and support you, to cheer you on, no matter what?"

Inevitably, the person we each promised to love forever won't be the same as they were the day you said, "I do." We'll both continue to change and (hopefully) grow. What does it mean to love each other with a consistency that says, "When everything else is changing, my love for your remains"? How do we cheer each other on through every win and loss?

Cheering each other on, for the two of us, means more than kind words. It looks different depending on the season of life, and it also depends on how we each feel cared for (um, not the same ways). For one of us it might be words of encouragement, time together, or taking something off their to-do list. One of the most important ways is just by showing up in their life and knowing what's happening in their world, who their friends are, what they care about. Those all matter. It's easy when we've been married awhile to get so caught up in parenting or work that we lose sight of that.

But while we might think about cheering on our spouse as something that happens behind the scenes, just the two of us, this fierce kind of love is not something we can do on our own. We were created to live in community with other people. It's important to have other couples we can be vulnerable with, because the reality is that what we might be walking through could be familiar territory for someone else.

For me (Jamie), it's been a struggle to bring friends into my marriage. Aaron's a pastor and most of our friends go to church with us. I don't want to share about a fight we're having and have my friends think poorly of their pastor. But when I expressed that concern to a friend, she responded that she and our other friends love Aaron as a brother in Christ. They want his health and wholeness.

That made me realize that as a family of God, we are all for each other, all cheering each other on. That helped me feel comfortable going to my girlfriends to process situations in my marriage and be a better partner to Aaron.

We've had to learn how to best support each other in each new season of life. We have to regularly ask, "How can I make sure you know that I am cheering for you and believe in you?" No one is perfect, but there's always something about your spouse you can highlight. Pointing out how you see them reflecting the image of God can bring so much unity, confidence, and joy into a marriage. Because we know at the end of the day, we're for each other, cheering each other on.

If we **LOVE** one another, God abides in us and His *love* is **PERFECTED** *in us.*

1 JOHN 4:12

Draw it out:

1. What is one thing you've noticed your spouse does well? Share it with them.

2. Ask your spouse, "What is one area I could better encourage you in?"

Pray together:

Reread 1 John 4:11-12. Take time to thank God for His steadfast love. Praise Him for creating humanity in His image, that we can experience God's beauty and love through one another. Ask God to help you journey with Him daily and grow in offering love and encouragement to your spouse.

Could You, for Once, Stop Being So Selfish?

By Leslie J. Barner

Do nothing from selfish ambition or conceit, but in humility count others more significant than yourselves. Let each of you look not only to his own interests but also to the interest of others.

PHILIPPIANS 2:3-4 (NIV)

On the first day of our honeymoon, I was so excited and proud to be Aubrey's wife that I was just plain giddy—to the point of being a bit, well . . . corny. I had this warm and loving feeling about us getting to take care of each other, serve each other, cherish each other. And I couldn't wait to put these feelings into practice. So I volunteered to unpack his suitcase and put things away for him while he checked out the awesome view of the beach on our balcony.

The first thing I took out of his suitcase was a pair of flip flops. I held those flip flops close to my chest and whispered, "These are *my* husband's flip flops." They felt special to me, because they were his, and he was mine. Yep! Corny!

From that day forward, it gave me so much joy to do things I thought would make him feel special, loved, and cherished. For instance, I made a practice of washing his clothes (not so sure he felt loved when I re-dyed a few pairs of his underwear as I learned you're not supposed to use bleach with colored clothes!). I cooked for him (took some time for me to master

DO NOTHING
FROM *selfish*
AMBITION.

PHILIPPIANS 2:3

this one too—I burned a pot of soup. Yikes!). And I loved making his plate and serving him, before serving myself.

He enjoyed serving me too. He made a practice of bringing me breakfast in bed on weekends (a favorite), helping with household chores, managing the finances (not my strength), helping with the children's homework, bath times, and bedtimes.

I was convinced we were both pretty selfless when it came to each other. Until I realized how selfish I had been in our marriage when, wait for it . . . we were planning our twenty-fifth wedding anniversary.

As we sat down to plan a vacation for our anniversary, I discovered Aubrey wanted to go on a cruise. That was the last thing I was interested in doing, for many reasons, most of them related to fears. I began talking about how much I'd love to go to an all-inclusive resort on a tropical island instead. It didn't take much to convince him to go along with my idea. He was used to doing the things I preferred to do. Every date we went on, every family activity, every vacation had always been where I wanted to go and what I wanted to do.

But then it hit me how selfish I had been. I realized how much joy it had brought him over the years to see me happy as we did all the things I wanted. I asked myself, "Could you, for once, stop being so selfish and do something he wants to do?" I was reminded that real love is not self-serving, nor does it insist on having its own way (1 Corinthians 13:4-8).

We went on that cruise. And he was all smiles the entire seven days, which brought me so much joy. It was one of our best vacations ever! We even renewed our vows on the ship, with the captain performing the ceremony. It was a special time that spoke love and value to my husband and drew us even closer together.

Selflessness is not easy for me, or the rest of us human beings. But in my marriage, selflessness is not only relationship-changing, it is a beautiful picture of Christ's sacrifice on the cross and His relationship with His Bride, the Church. It's a model of what a marriage should be.

The Apostle Paul draws this parallel in Ephesians 5:22–32. I am to lay down my life for Aubrey in the same way Jesus laid down His life for us. He died so we could experience the newness of life. In the same way, when I die to self in my marriage—which is something I have to practice every day—even when I don't feel like it, Aubrey and I can experience new life within our relationship ... one filled with unconditional love, togetherness, and hope.

IN HUMILITY

count others more

significant

than yourselves.

PHILIPPIANS 2:3-4 (NIV)

Draw it out:

1. When you and your spouse do things together, is it usually what you want to do? When was the last time you did something with your spouse that he or she wanted to do (even if it wasn't your thing)?

2. Share with each other some things you'd each like to do together.

3. Make two dates and take turns doing what you know will make your spouse feel happy and valued. Commit to making this a habit.

Pray together:

Ask God to examine your hearts and reveal any selfish behaviors you may be engaging in that are affecting your marriage, not only in the big things, but in the small things, too. Ask Him to help you put each other first by being attentive to each other's needs and interests. And pray for creative opportunities to serve each other in ways that speak value to each other and draw you closer together.

Running on Empty

By Bob Lepine

God's love has been poured into our hearts through the Holy Spirit who has been given to us.

ROMANS 5:5

Years ago, I was speaking at a marriage conference in Orlando. It was spring break for our kids, so we decided that after the conference was over, we would spend a few days together in central Florida. My wife, Mary Ann, would pack up the car and the kids and make the two-day drive from Arkansas. We'd all meet up, hit the theme parks, and have some family fun.

After traveling all day together in the car, Mary Ann and the kids reached Atlanta right at rush hour. Traffic was practically at a standstill, only going about four miles an hour. In the midst of that, our son, David, spilled his Jelly Bellies in the back seat of the car. He called out from the back, "Mom, I spilled my Jelly Bellies!"

With absolutely nothing in her reserve tank, Mary Ann just said, "There's no sympathy left for you!" The kids cracked up. In fact, it became one of the things we now say to one another in our family after a long day, "There's no sympathy left!"

Do you ever feel like that in your marriage? We've all had times when we're stressed out, depleted, with nothing in the reserve tank. And then something happens. Your spouse says or does something and you snap, "There's no margin left. No sympathy left here!"

How can you still love your spouse when your tank is empty?

GOD'S *love*

has been poured into our

HEARTS

through the Holy Spirit

who has been given to us.

ROMANS 5:5

If you're counting on the love you receive from your spouse to be the source of your love for them, you're in for trouble. You'll soon find yourself running on empty.

Here's why. Whether you know it or not, you have holes in your buckets. The love you receive from each other is a diminishing resource. You're going to run out before you know it. We know what happens to our cars when the tank is empty—it stalls out. It's not going anywhere. The same is true in our marriages, whenever someone spills the proverbial Jelly Bellies.

Fortunately, as Christians, Mary Ann and I have an infinite supply of love available to us. It's the love God has lavished on us. Romans 5:5 tells us He has poured His love into our hearts. His love is not scarce or limited. It's not dependent upon the love she and I receive from each other or anyone else for that matter. God's love never runs out.

In those times when Mary Ann and I feel like we don't have any love left to give , we can go back to God and say, "Fill me up again. I'm running on empty. I'm out of love. I'm out of capacity. I'm out of patience. I'm out of kindness. I'm out of all the things love is supposed to be. God, pour Your love into me, fill me up, and let me be a channel of Your love to my spouse."

Is this easy? No. Is this possible? Yes. It's possible when she and I put our hope in God. When we turn to God as our source, Isaiah 40:31 tells us, the Lord will renew your strength. You will soar on wings like eagles. You will run and not grow weary. You will walk and not be faint.

Next time there's no sympathy left in your marriage, cry out to God. Let Him fill you up. His love never runs out.

Draw it out:

1. How well do you love your spouse when your tank is empty?

2. What's one way you've seen your spouse love you when their tank is empty?

3. Commit Romans 5:5 and Isaiah 40:31 to memory. Pray and recite them the next time you're approaching empty.

Pray together:

Thank God for loving you and pouring out His love into your heart. Ask Him to forgive the times you've put the expectation of your tank being filled by your spouse. Ask God to continually fill you with His love and to give you gentle reminders that His abundant love is there and ready when you are empty. Praise Him for a love like this in your marriage.

Draw closer:

Proverbs 15:4 says a "gentle tongue is a tree of life." Often, the words slipping from our lips bring more strife than life. Consider your verbal influence by grabbing "The Power of Words" at FamilyLife.com/DrawnTogetherBonus.

Love in Action

By Andrea Griffith

> *In this the love of God was made manifest among us,*
> *that God sent his only Son into the world, so that we*
> *might live through him. In this is love, not that we have*
> *loved God but that he loved us and sent his son to be*
> *the propitiation for our sins. Beloved, if God so loved us,*
> *we also ought to love one another.*

1 JOHN 4:9-11

When our son, Zac, turned two, I decided to host a large birthday party. I don't know what gave me the idea that a two-year-old needed a large party. Maybe it was more about how I can't resist a fun reason to get everyone together.

The theme of the birthday party was baseballs and basketballs. I am not an avid cake decorator, but I had seen some easy to make cupcakes decorated to match the theme. I waited until the morning of the party to bake the cupcakes, which was the main reason I was running behind. As the cupcakes cooled, I made the different colored icings we would need and fed the icing into the decorating tubes and tips. Watching the clock tick by, I picked up my first cupcake only to realize I wasn't sure how to draw the lines to make it look like a basketball.

No worries, I thought. *My husband knows how to draw baseball and basketball lines. I'll just ask him to help. While he decorates the cupcakes, I'll decorate the table for the party and redeem the time.*

I walked into Trent's office where he was immersed in

writing and studying and asked if he would help me decorate the cupcakes. His reply left me crestfallen, "I am a man, and men do not decorate cakes." With my shoulders slumped, I hurried back into the kitchen to try to figure out how to make this work.

About five minutes later, Trent joined me in the kitchen. He picked up a cupcake and an icing tube. "What are you doing?" I asked.

"I'm decorating a cupcake," he said.

Pretty soon, Trent was immersed into cake decorating. He even attempted to write "Spalding" across the cupcakes. Amazed at this sudden change of heart, I asked him what happened.

He responded, "When you walked out of my office, the Holy Spirit walked in and asked me, 'Trent, do you love your wife?' 'Yes sir,' I said. 'Prove it!' God said." So he left his world of writing and studying to enter into my world of a two-year-old's birthday party.

Trent did on that day exactly what Jesus did and does for us every day. He loved me in a way that addressed the need of the hour.

When Jesus left His world, it was to address our deepest need. If He hadn't, we would never have had a way to the Father. Why did He do it? Because of love. Jesus communicated the love of the Father by entering our world. It was love that propelled Him to die for us and draw us back into His world.

Trent would be quick to say he has not left his world to enter mine nearly enough, but on this day, he profoundly reflected the love of Christ to me. We were able to work together to celebrate something significant in the life of our son. He had a very thankful wife more than willing to find ways to leave her world to join him in his.

BELOVED,

if God so loved us, we ought to

love one another.

1 JOHN 4:11

Draw it out:

1. Think of a time someone left their world and entered yours. How did that benefit you? How did it communicate love to you?

2. What is a practical way you can enter into your spouse's world today?

Pray together:

Thank the Lord that He left His world to enter into ours. Together, reflect on ways you both have felt Jesus' deep love for you. Ask for God's help today to love others well by entering into their worlds so that you, ultimately, point them to His.

Loving Smart

By Conway and Jada Edwards

"This is my commandment, that you love one another as I have loved you."

JOHN 15:12

There we were ... just looking at each other in the kitchen and thinking, *Somebody needs to make the food.*

I (Jada) was thinking, *I cooked three days in a row, isn't it your turn?* But Conway's thoughts were, *I don't understand this "turn" word you're using.*

Neither one of us understood what in the world the other was thinking. Neither of us understood why the other didn't think they should cook. But both of us stood strong in our conviction that we were not going to pick up a single pot or pan in that kitchen.

But let's rewind and share a little background of how we ended up in this kitchen standoff.

My (Conway) mom grew up where the husband was the king of the home, so my mom has served my dad all the days of his life. Meaning, this morning he had breakfast laid out for him at their home in Jamaica. No questions asked. So coming into marriage, I had the expectation that Jada would do the same thing my mom did. No questions asked.

Jada, on the other hand, had a completely different experience in her family. Her dad did all the cooking, and he did all the domestic work. No questions asked.

"This is my commandment,

THAT YOU *love one another* as I have LOVED YOU."

JOHN 15:12

When we got married, both of us were looking for some-body to serve us based on our upbringing and what we saw modeled by our parents. This led us to always debating, think-ing, *Okay, it's your turn. When are you going to serve me?*

Which ultimately led to that kitchen standoff—both of us starving and neither of us knowing where to go from there. Thankfully, we've both grown a lot since that day, both in serving and loving one another.

For me (Conway), loving Jada meant understanding her family of origin. I needed to figure out what her needs were, just like Christ does for me. And I needed to determine how to love her in the ways she desired to be loved. (And serving each other goes far beyond household tasks.)

This was extraordinarily challenging early in our marriage, and it is still challenging to this day. I have to continually figure out what Jada needs in a husband, based on what the Word of God says, what her needs are, and what she experienced in her family of origin. That's a lot. It has been a journey, maybe one that you are on as well.

When you think about loving your spouse well, the emotional feelings can come a little easier. You go into marriage knowing this person meets some criteria: they make you feel a certain way, they help you accomplish one of life's goals . . . whatever the case may be. But for me (Jada), loving well has often been about loving *smart*.

Loving smart is educating myself on Conway. Early in our marriage, someone told us, "Listen, you have a PhD in your life—knowing who you are, how you think, and what you love. And I don't care if you've lived with your spouse before. I don't care if you've dated since you were twelve. You still have a kindergarten education on that person, because they're not *you*."

No matter how long you've known your spouse, loving smart is being a student of the one God gave you. The better we know our spouses, the better we can love them. That is probably one of the hardest things. Right when we think we've got it, we can find out we haven't been doing well or their needs change; it's a constant learning process.

For us, knowing each other's family of origin was huge. Our sets of parents were very different people, and they had very different roles in the home. We still have to take that into consideration and work through these expectations when loving each other.

It's not easy, but loving smart has been a worthwhile effort that has fundamentally changed our marriage ... for the better.

Draw it out:

1. On a scale of one to ten, how well do you know your spouse?

2. Take turns discussing one thing you don't understand about the other person but would like to better understand.

3. How can you make learning more about each other a regular part of loving smart in your home?

Pray together:

Thank the Lord He knows and loves you deeper than anyone. And thank Him for giving you one another, so you can have another person to know well and love well in this life. Ask Him to help you always seek to learn more about Him and one another, so you can love smart and love well.

Why Marriage Hurts So Good

By Justin Talbert

Husbands, love your wives, as Christ loved the church and gave himself up for her, that he might sanctify her, having cleansed her by the washing of water with the word, so that he might present the church to himself in splendor, without spot or wrinkle or any such thing, that she might be holy and without blemish. In the same way husbands should love their wives as their own bodies. He who loves his wife loves himself.

EPHESIANS 5:25-28

Isn't it amazing that when we walk into a gym, we expect pain? And it's not just that we expect it, we *embrace* it. "Ah," we grunt. "It hurts so good!" In fact, we'd venture that the litmus test of a good "gym experience" is the amount of pain our bodies endured.

Pain is gain, after all.

But isn't it even more amazing (or puzzling) that when we walk into marriage, we expect ease? Suddenly, pain is lame.

Just to be real, my wife and I noticed recently that our screentime graphs on our phones have *skyrocketed* in "hours per week" (it's hard to argue with a literal graph). With the kids finally down to bed, the evening's default has become an individually pixelated entertainment session. Seems harmless, right? That's what we thought. Until we started digging in and found two points of contention—intimacy and grudge-holding—were lurking beneath our actions.

Rather than leaning into these issues with a heart to re-solve them, we were fleeing to easier terrain: our phones, ca-tered to our preferences of comfort and self-indulgence. We'd like to see those graphs plummet in the next month or two, and for us to enter the "pain" of real-life issues we've been avoiding. But it's gonna hurt.

So, let's roll up our sleeves and re-examine a classic Scripture on marriage, paying close attention to the verbs. Ephesians 5:25-28 says, "Husbands, *love* your wives, as Christ *loved* the church and gave himself up for her, that he might *sanctify* her, *having cleansed* her by the washing of water with the word, so that he might *present* the church to himself in splendor, without spot or wrinkle or any such thing, that she might *be holy and without blemish.* In the same way husbands should *love* their wives as their own bodies."

Marriage demands dying to sin, which means pain (pushing us far outside of our comfort zones, examining those parts of us we'd rather hide) . . . which leads to gain (not lame).

Practically, this dying to sin involves both the vertical and horizontal plane. Individually, both spouses are pursuing holiness—becoming more Christlike—on their own. But what's often overlooked is at the horizontal level, you are linking arms with your spouse to help fight *their* sin. And they're helping to fight *yours.* Notice it isn't a "me vs. you" thing. It has nothing to do with pointing fingers and shame. It is an alliance, a team: You and your spouse versus sin.

While the pain of the gym strengthens the muscles, the pain of marriage strengthens holiness. Sin is exposed, confronted, killed. No other work, play, or relationship ensures this holiness, because nothing else involves the union, oneness, and intimate community of marriage.

We all know this because we experience it. We feel it. Your spouse is probably the best and worst person you know, because you know him/her the best. There's a lot of sin there. Which makes the union incredibly messy at times, but that should've been our expectation from the start: that the Lord uses your spouse to sanctify you, and you to sanctify your spouse. Which sounds like the worst thing ever *until* you remember what bookends the verses above: *agape* love, an unconditional and sacrificial love.

If you or your spouse tends to flee toward other activities at the first sighting of difficulty in marriage (even subconsciously, see also: phones), creating a culture of agape love allows a safety net for you to move back toward each other, slaying the sin that threatened to pull you apart. To just be loved without conditions is what agape love is all about. Who doesn't want more of that?

It's compelling. It is *more* than compelling, it's where Jesus is. This sort of gospel experience is so beautiful and rare and unnatural that it's irresistibly other-worldly. It's ... heavenly.

When you, in agape love, labor to see your spouse become more like Jesus, you're free to appropriately confront their sin. But it's never naggy or better than thou. It's like the gym. You and your spouse aren't "out to get each other." You're laying yourself down for each other. More, you're opening up yourself to the other, in arguably the most vulnerable way. But it's all good, because you are both committed to upping the other's holiness—to see them more like Jesus. In love.

Which hurts, sure. But it hurts so good.

Draw it out:

1. Where do you tend to "flee" when marriage gets difficult?

2. How might viewing conflict as an opportunity to kill sin shift the way you handle conflict?

3. Why does your pursuit of holiness feel safer when it's surrounded by agape love in marriage?

Pray together:

Ask God to give you perspective and grace in the midst of conflict to see your sin, to confess your sin, and to kill your sin. And for your spouse to do the same. Pray that marriage difficulty won't lead to pursuing other things as priority over marriage.

LUO

The biblical word luo is flexible in its various meanings, but that does not make it weak. If you're wanting to untie a knot, transgress a law (bad idea!), or put an end to something—luo is your word. You can cut off, separate, or free something. The gospel itself can be summarized using this word. We've all "luo'd" God's law in that we have transgressed or untied it. But Jesus has "luo'd" our sin: He has *taken it away*. He has essentially untied our untying!

One way to bring this gospel-saturated word into marriage is when you consider your spouse's sin. Their sin is like a knot, isn't it? Instead of blame-shifting your poor reactions onto their knot of sin, what if you took on the ministry of unraveling with them that knot . . . through undeserved kindness? We often speak of bearing each other's burdens. Is unraveling another's sin not included?

A Debt-Free Marriage

By Conway and Jada Edwards

"Judge not, and you will not be judged; condemn not, and you will not be condemned; forgive, and you will be forgiven; give, and it will be given to you. Good measure, pressed down, shaken together, running over, will be put into your lap. For with the measure you use it will be measured back to you."

LUKE 6:37-38

Many marriage fights and marriage failures are, in part, due to finances. Money—a lack of it or how it's spent—is a common tension in relationships. And several studies have shown most couples believe having debt is a reason to consider divorce. Being in financial bondage can be a problem and a major marriage killer.

But there's another type of debt quietly resulting in the isolation of couples and often leading to divorce: the debt of unforgiveness. When we don't forgive our spouses for their offenses or for the pain they caused, and we hold a grudge, it can result in a constant "you owe me" method of operation. We've been guilty of this in our own marriage.

When one of us thinks the other wronged us, we want to use it against them so they can feel some of the pain we're feeling. Yet the gospel teaches us that when we were at our worst, Christ forgave us: ". . . but God shows his love for us in that while we were still sinners, Christ died for us" (Romans 5:8). So, instead of holding onto unforgiveness for our worst offenses and mistakes, we're called to love and consistently pursue each other like God pursues us.

But that doesn't make it easy.

It helps us to think of unforgiveness in our marriage like a bank account. We both start at zero. Each time one of us offends the other, the offender loses "currency," or in this case, owes the other something. But when we forgive each other, that negative balance goes back to zero.

When we withhold forgiveness for past arguments, we often come into the next one already at a deficit. This is not a healthy place to work from. The hole of unforgiveness continues to get deeper and deeper. Like financial debt, it's hard to climb out when you continue to add more debt before the original is paid off. And if you've ever been in financial debt, you know how it can negatively impact every aspect of your life.

The exact same feelings of despair and helplessness can be the result of unforgiveness in our marriages as it continues to mount. And it can be hard for us to see our way out.

Often, what we need is a reset: forgiving each other from the debt we've accumulated along the way. But don't be mistaken here. Forgiveness doesn't mean the offense is erased, nor does it mean we forget it. It does mean we have to let go of wanting the other to feel the pain we experienced. It means we release our spouses from owing us anything, so that we have a healthy place to work from in addressing the issue. And yes, unless it is an insignificant offense, the issue needs to be calmly worked through so that healing and reconciliation can take place. Forgiveness is a critical part of that process so that when we make our next mistake (and we will!), we're not still paying for the last ones.

Just like relieving your financial burden isn't easy, this takes time and a "debt-free" mindset. We have to go back to our relationship with Jesus Christ, recalling how He forgave us and gave us the same ability to forgive others—especially our spouses. Luke 6:37-38 serves as a reminder: "Judge not, and you will not be judged; condemn not, and you will not be condemned; forgive, and you will be forgiven; give, and it will be given to you. Good measure, pressed down, shaken together, running over, will be put into your lap. For with the measure you use it will be measured back to you."

This frees us from a "you owe me" relationship and moves us toward a marriage that models the gospel. God doesn't require us to do anything to receive His gift of forgiveness. We just have to accept it. He paid our debt, and we can receive that freedom today. No strings attached. What an amazing gift! A gift that is not just for us to have on the receiving end, but to also offer on the giving end.

Draw it out:

1. Why is it harder to grant forgiveness than to hold onto a grudge?

2. What's one thing you can do today to take the first step toward a "debt-free" marriage?

3. Imagine and discuss what marriage and life will be like when you are debt-free, continually forgiving and loving each other.

Pray together:

Thank God for His endless love and forgiveness and for sending Jesus so that you can be debt-free. Ask for His help in not harboring unforgiveness in your heart toward your spouse. Ask that He would empower you to love your spouse the way He loves you.

In This Corner: Team Us

By Candice Colclough

> *For we do not wrestle against flesh and blood, but against the rulers, against the authorities, against the cosmic powers over this present darkness, against the spiritual forces of evil in the heavenly places.*

EPHESIANS 6:12

"In the right corner, we have The Wife—standing five foot four, wearing pink and yellow. In the left corner, you have The Husband—standing six foot one, wearing blue and white. We are here for the marriage fight of the century, so let's *goooo!"*

Harold and I have found ourselves across from each other in the ring way too many times in the battles we face. Our expectations, parenting, finances, career decisions, and even the small, day-to-day life choices can outweigh our love and respect. We go about life the wrong way.

But we had to realize we are stronger on the same side of the ring.

Ecclesiastes 4:9-12 reminds us, "Two are better than one, because they have a good reward for their toil. For if they fall, one will lift up his fellow. But woe to him who is alone when he falls and has not another to lift him up! Again, if two lie together, they keep warm, but how can one keep warm alone? And though a man might prevail against one who is alone, two will withstand him—a threefold cord is not quickly broken."

Two are definitely better than one. Two tires on a bike are much easier. Two working headlights are much more useful.

Two graham crackers for your s'mores taste much better. Two pilots are wiser. You can most definitely make it by with just one, but two gives you a more balanced, brighter, sweeter, and safer outcome. Countless are the benefits from choosing to fight on the same side.

Marriage acts as God's example to the world of what love, grace, and mercy look like. And being on the same team in marriage is a true illustration of that love. Good teammates are neither boastful or envious; they are not arrogant or rude. Neither teammate will insist on pushing only their way. A good teammate isn't irritable or resentful. This team bears all things, endures all things (1 Corinthians 13:4-8).

So, for example, what does a winning team look like in parenting?

Harold and I have a double-blended family. When we got married, I had a daughter, and Harold had a son. Then together, we had two more children. And I don't know about y'all, but our kiddos can smell any discord amongst their parents. They each have their own idea of what we should give them permission for and when or how long we should discipline them. If we aren't on the same team on these issues, they will definitely take advantage. Two parents on the same team are a lot more effective than two parents with separate agendas.

So what does a winning team look like when it comes to day-to-day life?

One way is deciding our family calendar. We've plowed through many stages in our marriage, but one of the hardest was when our calendars were dictated by our individual desires as opposed to Team Us. Hobbies and friends occupied our time. My husband was all about video games; I was all about being at church. Which sounds good in theory... but how much time I spent there, hanging out with friends, was unfair to our family.

Harold and I both had to step back and assess our mutual priorities. We had to realign our desires and time with Christ and each other. This wasn't easy, but it was definitely worth it. With four kiddos, two working parents, and ministry, making time for each other and functioning as a team is so much better for all of us.

When we are on the same team, what the enemy wants to separate is impossible (Mark 10:9). And when we are on the same side of the ring, we remember that our fight is not against each other. "For we do not wrestle against flesh and blood, but against the rulers, against the authorities, against the cosmic powers over this present darkness, against the spiritual forces of evil in the heavenly places" (Ephesians 6:12).

Our fight is **NOT** against *each other.*

Draw it out:

1. What areas of your marriage or life do you find more difficult to approach as a team?

2. What makes it difficult for you to trust your spouse to be your equal teammate?

Pray together:

Thank God for your differences and similarities. Ask for His help to remember that being on the same team is how He designed marriage to look. Ask that your teamwork would mirror God's love to those around you. And when you are struggling to arrive on the same page, ask Him to remind you that the fight is not against each other.

The Unraveling Marriage

By Justin Talbert

> *If we say we have no sin, we deceive ourselves, and the truth is not in us. If we confess our sins, he is faithful and just to forgive us our sins and to cleanse us from all unrighteousness.*

1 JOHN 1:8-9

I love watching people's eyebrows furrow when I say there are three words more important in marriage than "I love you." (Did yours just furrow?)

After a deliberate, albeit dramatic pause, I continue, "The three words more important than 'I love you' are 'I am sorry.'" Without fail, the person pauses to ponder, then nods, as if to say, "I can get on board with that."

Though the importance of each could be up for debate, there's truth to this idea. We all know the magic of an apology, of turning back from going the wrong way. There is such flowering health in reviewing an action and rightly dubbing it wrong. We might go so far as to say that for love to be genuine, for the "I love you" to hold its meaning, apologies are necessary. Otherwise, there's an evergreen eye roll and perpetual wound.

The arduousness of "I am sorry" also holds its magic. We've all been there. You're arguing with your spouse, conflict is heightening, you know you're out-of-bounds at this point— pulse is heightened, body is stiffened, words are venomous. But you simply can't say, "I'm sorry . . ." It's much easier to double-down, save face, get that last sting, bring up that last shred of evidence to further your argument.

The whole situation feels like a knot: tightening, weaving further intricacies into itself both immovable and suffocating. You're beyond the words "I love you." Or so it feels that way. You're beyond the words "I am sorry." Or so it feels that way. An acidic coating is added to the knot of your heart, the knot of your conflict.

Only three words untie that knot. You're already mouthing them, aren't you?

"I am sorry."

Those of us who follow Jesus understand grace: God's unmerited kindness. But has grace seeped so deeply into your inner being that you can gain perspective even when tied up by conflict? Christians are the best equipped to not take our "rightness" too seriously. We know just how wrong we can be (and are). Because we understand what it took to make us right: slaughter of the second Person of the Trinity.

We can't strut about in self-righteousness. We can't think ourselves above our spouse. We know from where we started, what we deserve, and the insidious flesh we still battle.

Last Thursday, I snapped at my wife, May. I'd just gotten home from work and was expecting a phone call. The kids (three boys between five and eight years old) were treating the living room like a playground. Wifey was rattling off plans for the evening, tasks to get done, and something about her workout from that morning. I just gave it the old, lazy, dismissive, "That's great, just give me a sec." It had a little poison in it.

She snapped one back, quite stressed herself, finishing with, "Don't take your day out on me." I responded, "I'm not!" like an idiot. The funny thing is, I believed my own words for a second. She huffed and returned to whatever she was doing.

Picture this scene as a knot. You sensed it tightening, right? Becoming more intricate, more complicated, more suffocating. How does the knot loosen? Not by doubling

down! The knot started unraveling when, in God's grace, I took personal inventory, named my stress, and realized I was an idiot. I walked over to May and said, "I'm sorry. I did take out the day on you."

Freeze. This was a crucial moment. I did my role. But a knot takes two ends of a rope, so what May did next was important. It would have been easy for her to say, "Yeah, you did. You're the worst. Idiot!" But she didn't. May received my words, looked me in the eye, took a breath, and said, "Forgiven. I snapped, too. Go on, tell me about your day."

A knot loosens quicker than it ties if you know where to pull.

Practically, it's all about self-forgetfulness. Again, picture your fleshly, demanding, devising, selfish self like a gigantic knot. In this moment, you forget yourself for the sake of your spouse. The alternative, of course, is to continue living for self: protecting, hedging, justifying.

But when we, like Jesus and in Jesus, "do nothing from selfish ambition or conceit, but in humility count others more significant than ourselves" (Philippians 2:3), we can lower ourselves in humility and say those most blessed words, "I am sorry."

This is the new self, where matchless joy flows from undeserved humility. It's Christian marriage. It's untying and turning back.

The magic of an apology is that in those three words, you're actually saying all six.

He is

faithful

& JUST

to forgive us our sins

and to cleanse us

from all unrighteousness.

1 JOHN 1:8

Draw it out:

1. What's one barrier between you and confessing your wrongs to your spouse during conflict?

2. In light of the gospel, why is it ironic for Christians to continually justify their rightness?

3. What is scary and beautiful about self-forgetfulness?

Pray together:

Praise God for the cross, where the weight of His love and our sin meet, which enables our forgiveness. Ask God to help you confess your sins quicker than your spouse and for you to forgive your spouse quicker and quicker as the years unfold.

Love and Conflict Coexist

By D.A. and Elicia Horton

> *But God shows his love for us in that while we were still sinners, Christ died for us.*
>
> ROMANS 5:8

We were once asked the question, "How does conflict, when done right, actually bring you together instead of tear you apart?"

A lot of people feel a marriage that has conflict is not a good marriage. And if the two of us were asked this question early in our marriage, the answer would have been, "It can't. Conflict doesn't bring you together. Conflict and love can't coexist."

I (D.A.) used to be in that camp. I believed when there was conflict or disappointment, love was lacking. Truth be told, when we were arguing and attempting to resolve conflict in wrong or unhealthy ways, we were both more prone to look at things from our own vantage point. This vantage point gave us a very limited view of the big picture of our marriage and family and how we were doing.

Even years into marriage, "little Damon," my younger, not as mature self, still existed inside of me. The little boy in me felt that when Elicia was disappointed in me, she didn't love me anymore. It put me in the mindset that my performance had to earn her approval and love. This left me exhausted! I'd do everything I could to keep her happy and avoid any type of conflict. All I wanted was for her to not be mad at me, because "little Damon" believed she couldn't be mad at me and love me at the same time.

In order for us to see the whole panoramic view, it's helpful to walk and talk through all the triggers that led to our moment of conflict. Those triggers can include anything in our lives—from work to kids, to the rhythms and busyness of being two parents working full-time, with a limited amount of time. Nothing is off-limits.

Working through conflict together has allowed me to grow to mature, grown Damon who knows Elicia loves me even when disappointed in me.

Conflict brings attention to an issue in my life or marriage in the same way a highlighter brings attention to words in a book. You can't just gloss over it. You have to pause, maybe even reread it. You might need to note something about it which resonates with you or reveals something you never knew. For D.A. and me (Elicia), this could be in our communication, our oneness, or just in areas where he and I are two totally different people. But the highlighted words are assumed to be important. When we realize this, it brings a shift in the way we handle conflict.

For one, this has helped us realize being different isn't bad. Instead, being different can help us appreciate each other's perspective and grow in that area. It helped me (Elicia) go from fighting to be understood to having a heart that wants to understand. This was key for me, as it tempered my frustrations and put them back in alignment with God's heart.

Love & conflict

can coexist.

This led to so many "aha" moments that we often said, "Why didn't we talk about this in the beginning?!"

We've found that coexistent conflict and love require shifts in perspective, habit changes, and a lot of understanding. But this results in so much growth, maturity, love, and appreciation for one another and our marriage.

The next time you're fearing or avoiding conflict, try saying to yourself, "love and conflict can coexist." Recognize it as important enough to work through. Think about it in relation to the big picture of your marriage and family. Then prayerfully work through it, expecting to grow closer as a result.

Draw it out:

1. What first came to mind when you read the words, "love and conflict can coexist"?

2. Up to this point, what has been your default response when you are faced with conflict?

3. Next time conflict arises, how can you approach resolving it in a healthy way?

Pray together:

Thank God that despite the mistakes you make and actions you take which may disappoint Him, He still loves you. Confess to Him any areas where you don't always show the same love to your spouse when disappointed or when having differing perspectives. Ask Him to align your heart with His so you can love your spouse in the same way God loves you. Then praise God for using conflict as a catalyst for love, not a barrier.

Why You Should Fight in Public

By Jonathan "JP" Pokluda

> *And let us consider how to stir up one another to love and good works, not neglecting to meet together, as is the habit of some, but encouraging one another...*

HEBREWS 10:24-25

"You're not going to coach her up, man. So, stop trying!"

Those are the words my good friend shared with me after witnessing a public fight between my wife, Monica, and me. And that wasn't the only fight we've had in public. This may sound weird, but I'm grateful we fight in public. I think you should do the same.

You may be thinking, *Wait, are you actually encouraging me to fight with my spouse in public? To air out our dirty laundry and hash out our differences in public?* Yes and no. Here's what I mean.

We've brought our community into our arguments. Our community being the people we love, who love us and God, and who deeply care about us and our marriage. The people we do life with. In this community, there have been living room conversations with mascara running down Monica's face and times when I've been really worked up. But when people who care about us have seen and observed it, they've been able to help by offering a safe, outside perspective.

I needed to hear those words from my friend that day. They were life-changing to my marriage. Had he not been brought into our fight, he would have never been able to tell me to put the brakes on coaching up (or "correcting," if you know what I mean) my wife.

I know the idea of resolving conflict in the context of community, even close community, can be terrifying. But this concept of community has changed my life and my marriage more than anything other than Jesus.

Initially, Monica and I felt like we didn't have a choice of when or where we had conflict. It seemed like when we were together—whether people were there or not—we ended up in some sort of argument. Maybe you feel the same, like you don't have a choice. Or maybe you will do anything and everything you can to avoid having conflict in front of anyone, even those closest to you.

For us, it's something we actually invite. There've been times we were in a proverbial ditch and couldn't get out. So we called a few people and said, "Hey, can you come over and help us? We need a mediator." We needed someone to help us see our individual parts or roles in the conflict. We realized we were so entrenched in it, we couldn't see past our own thoughts and opinions. So we invited our community in.

Yes, this concept of community can be scary. It might be hard to imagine saying anything that might paint us in a

...consider how to stir up one another to *Love* & good works...

HEBREWS 10:24

negative picture to someone else, but let me encourage you to push through that. As you begin to experience healing, I believe you will long for it.

Think of your child having a splinter. They're terrified when you come with the tweezers to pull it out. Your child says, "No, no, no, I don't want you to. It hurts, it hurts, it hurts!" But as a loving parent, you know when you get that splinter out, healing can take place. In our marriages, we can be like a child with a splinter, saying, "No, no, no, I can't, I can't. You don't understand. I can't fight in public!" But if you do, I believe you're going to experience life-giving healing in your marriage.

You will have conflict in your marriage the rest of your life; it is inevitable. Knowing this, you have two options. You can get to the end of your marriage (or your life) and realize you had a miserable marriage because you never really faced your fears, got help, and worked at it in the right ways. Or you can courageously face those fears, invite others in to help, and have an amazing marriage.

We chose the second option, and I can honestly say we have an amazing marriage—even though we've experienced some of the worst things you might experience in marriage. This came by inviting others in, pursuing the truth of the Scripture, and truly surrendering to the Holy Spirit's work through both. You, too, have access to help from both His Holy Spirit and a community of like-minded people who walk alongside you. It's a choice that'll change your marriage forever.

Draw it out:

1. Identify the people in your life who love God the most and say, "Will you meet me at _____ on a specific day/time/week?" Ask them to meet consistently with the intent of spurring each other on toward love and good deeds.

2. When you meet, take turns answering the following questions and praying for one another: How did you feed your soul this week? How did you feed others? And how did you feed your flesh?

3. With your spouse, identify couples who love God the most and do something similar to the aforementioned. Ask them to meet monthly with you as a couple, rotating homes/hosts. Each time you meet, take turns answering the following questions and praying for one another. How did you feed your marriage? How did you feed your spouse? And how did you hurt your marriage?

Pray together:

Read Hebrews 10:24-25 together. Ask God to reveal (or bring) people and couples who can be this type of community for you and provide accountability. Thank Him for not leaving you alone to fight for your marriage, and praise Him for a marriage worth fighting for.

Wait, What Are We Fighting About?

By Aaron and Jamie Ivey

So if there is any encouragement in Christ, any comfort from love, any participation in the Spirit, any affection and sympathy, complete my joy by being of the same mind, having the same love, being in full accord and of one mind.

PHILIPPIANS 2:1-2

Early on in our marriage, I (Aaron) found myself just trying to win any argument with Jamie rather than trying to listen, empathize, or even understand why there was a conflict. We'd stop in the middle of a fight like, "Wait, what are we fighting about?" And I'd think, *I don't actually remember, but I know I'm so mad right now.*

I (Jamie) was the same way. In those moments, both of us had to rewind and ask: do we know what we're fighting for? Are we fighting for our own desires, or are we entering into conflict to help us better understand each other? We might disagree, but we need to fight for—not against—each other. My spouse is not my enemy, right? Both of us have to seek to serve and love the other person. It's hard work, and sometimes, it's easier to try to win this fight with rhetoric or a good defense, but we've each had to lay that down and recognize unity is more important than winning.

Twenty years into marriage, our fights look a lot different than they did in the beginning. (Whew.) I (Aaron) am less of a conflict-avoider now. In difficult seasons, I still tend to want to go into a cave to figure it all out—so I can come back out of the cave with a plan to fix everything.

My (Jamie) default pattern when conflict arises is to automatically assume the worst. My insecurities come out. *Maybe Aaron doesn't love me anymore. Maybe our marriage is on the brink of divorce.* I want Aaron to be my knight in shining armor and save everything. That causes a lot of additional conflict.

Jamie's had to learn that I (Aaron) cannot complete her. I've had to learn she also doesn't need me to have a solution or a perfect plan.

Over the years, we've come to view conflict as an opportunity to grow closer. For me (Jamie) to believe this, I have to trust conflict doesn't mean we're over but that we get to work through something together. And I (Aaron) need to be gracious and tender in how I bring conflict to Jamie.

We've learned to talk through conflict and not try to resolve it in a limited timeframe. People say to never go to sleep without finishing an argument, but sometimes, we have to pause for the night and say, "Hey, I love you. We're not going to fix this tonight. I'm for you. Let's talk again tomorrow." When we rest on it, we can more clearly see the conflict and work through it faster.

In the old days, two kings or warriors would shake hands before working through conflict. This was to acknowledge they had something to work through, but also to show they weren't holding any weapons. They weren't coming to inflict more damage but to find resolution.

This offers a beautiful picture of how we can approach conflict in marriage. We can come to each other with humble hearts and say, "I don't want to wound you anymore. There might be something that's hard for you to hear, but I'm not coming with any weapons. I just want us to be able to say what we need to say and come closer together."

All of us tend to enter conflict with a weapon in our hand. My (Aaron's) weapon of choice has always been words. I was a communication major in college, so I learned how to debate and prove my point. But engaging in conflict in a healthy way means laying down your weapons—with open hands and aiming for reconciliation.

In Philippians 2:3-4, Paul writes to do everything in humility, just as Christ humbly laid down His life for us. That concept feels difficult in marriage. It doesn't seem fair to enter an argument with humility when we feel the other person is in the wrong. But when we consider what it looks like to follow Christ and walk in the words of Scripture, it changes the reason and the way she and I argue. No longer are we fighting for our own needs, wants, and desires. Now we're fighting for us. Sometimes, fighting for "us" means that I don't get to say the seventh point, I just get to apologize to my spouse. It's a shift in thinking to have humility in an argument.

When we're tempted to bring up old tendencies or assume we're right, Jamie and I can choose to demand our own way or choose the way of Christ: humility, love, and servanthood. With practice and encouragement from one another, we've seen conflict not as a problem to rush through but an opportunity to follow Christ in humble servanthood and grow closer to each other.

Draw it out:

1. In what ways was Jesus a humble servant?

2. What weapon might you need to lay down to walk in the way of Christ?

3. What is one way God might be using conflict to grow you closer to your spouse?

Pray together:

Reread Philippians 2:1-2. Thank God for the help and comfort He gives, so that we can lay down our weapons when disagreeing with our spouses and others. Praise Him for being a God of love and reconciliation. Ask Him to teach you to approach arguments with humility. Pray that each conflict would help you to better understand and love your spouse.

COMPLETE

my joy by being

of the **same mind,**

having the same *love,*

being in full accord and of

ONE MIND.

PHILIPPIANS 2:2

Pause, Pray, Proceed

By Chris and Alisa Grace

> *For it is God who works in you, both to will and to work for his good pleasure.*

PHILIPPIANS 2:13

I (Chris) think anger is an amazingly helpful emotion. It tells me what's going on in my heart. Anger really is this insight into my soul. If I learn to see anger as information about what's going on in my heart and not just something to be fixed, I can use it for the good of my marriage.

A great verse I (Alisa) try to keep in mind is Philippians 2:13. It says, "for God is at work" giving us two things: 1) the desire to do His will and 2) the power to do what pleases Him. If God has called us to be loving, humble, appreciative, kind, and forgiving to each other, then He's going to give us the ability to do it.

But without thinking about it, I'm just going to decide to always speak with kindness, be quick to listen and forgive, and be slow to get angry when conflict arises with Chris—all in my own power. I know I'm supposed to do all those things, but when push comes to shove, I can't do it.

A principle Chris and I try to practice in the middle of conflict is to pause, pray, and then proceed. When things are getting heated, we want to call a timeout and spend some time apart in prayer. We do this because when we feel overwhelmed by anger or the tension of an argument, it can create emotional flooding. Our heart rates, body temperatures, and respiration rates increase because our bodies are going into "fight or flight" mode. He and I begin to look at each other as somebody to fight rather than someone we can work with to process our feelings.

That's when we've each found we need to pause so we can pray, cry, go for a walk, or simply sit there and process what's happening inside. The temptation is to ruminate and rehearse the pain and anger, but what we need in those moments is to reflect on our own hearts and give each other the benefit of the doubt. *What deeper emotional button is getting pushed right now? Where do I need to ask the Lord to start the healing process? What work do God and I need to do together?*

As we pause, we can bring all of what we're feeling to the Lord in prayer. There's something profoundly personal about the fact that God knows us so well He knows each tear. Maybe you're not a crier, but you can still take time to pause and reflect with the Lord. Trust us: Conflict can be an opportunity *for* your relationship, rather than something to work *against* your relationship.

Research shows it takes twenty minutes for our bodies to return to normal patterns after we experience emotional flooding. And Chris and I have experienced that once our emotions have come back down, we're able to better listen and articulate what's going on in our hearts.

When we're ready to proceed, the first step is to offer a genuine apology. When I (Chris) start to apologize then bring up something Alisa did, I'm not taking full responsibility for my part. Or we can ruin apologies when we use the phrase, "Well, I'm sorry you feel that way." Again, it's not taking ownership of your part in the conflict. It's almost like saying, "I'm sorry you responded so unreasonably to my perfectly reasonable action." Then, once we've sought forgiveness from the Lord and our spouse, it's time to forgive ourselves and release the situation.

As we share insights from our time with the Lord, we're giving our spouse access to a much deeper place in our hearts. I (Alisa) may still have some woundedness, but Chris can be a part of the healing the Lord does in my heart. And I can do the same for him. It's a great way to be a conduit of God's grace to each other. Conflict opens the door to our ability to understand the deep recesses of another person.

For our marriage to grow, Chris and I have to cultivate the perfect soil in which to deal with hard things. We had to learn what it means to take some of the weeds of our sin and brokenness out in order to create a safe place for things like nourishment, love, and joy to grow. And it's in that safe place that a couple is able to work through conflict and allow God to do His work in you both.

Pause. Pray. Proceed.

PAUSE
pray
PROCEED

Draw it out:

1. When a situation gets intense, do you usually resort to fight mode, or flight mode?

2. The next time an argument gets heated, what step could you take to pause and process your emotions with the Lord?

3. What are some of the "nutrients" that amend your marriage's soil toward emotional safety for you and your spouse? How could you invite the Holy Spirit into your marriage as you cultivate these?

Pray together:

Reread Philippians 2:13. Thank God that you don't have to try to do everything in your own power. Praise Him for giving you all you need to do His will. Ask God to guide you in the power of the Holy Spirit both during conflict and in your marriage as a whole.

When It's Okay to Keep Score

By Tim Muehlhoff

Whoever refreshes others will be refreshed.

PROVERBS 11:25, NIV

I remember a time when my wife and I were in a funk in our marriage. We just felt everything seemed negative, and we couldn't figure out what was going on. But as we began to peel back the layers of those negative feelings, we realized neither of us were feeling appreciated by the other. So we decided to do something which felt a little awkward.

At least once a day, we committed to saying one thing we appreciated about the other person. It had to be genuine. It couldn't just be, "Hey, you weren't such a jerk today. Like, thanks for that." As we implemented this daily practice we began intentionally looking for and pointing out the positive in each other.

A friend of mine once offered an invaluable piece of advice: Catch your spouse doing what's right. We put their advice into practice by training ourselves to look at the positive in each other, reminding us of those attributes we really enjoyed and appreciated. It helped us rebuild a culture of appreciation, which had slowly broken down over time. And fairly quickly, maybe within a couple of weeks, we started to notice more and more positives. It became easier to notice them.

The key wasn't just noticing them but expressing them. I couldn't just think, *I really appreciated when my wife did this;* I had to actually write it down and share it with her.

The simple practice of noticing and articulating what we appreciate about each other is rooted in a key observation by John Gottman,[2] a well-known marriage expert. Gottman says one of the best ways couples can improve their relationship is by developing a five-to-one ratio of positive interactions to negative interactions. Each positive doesn't have to be this major expression. It just needs to be anything that is a positive influence in the marriage.

At first, Gottman's ratio can be confusing. Why five-to-one? Doesn't that seem like overkill? You'd think if I have one positive interaction to one negative interaction, then everything should balance out. That should keep us in pretty good shape, right? If not one-to-one, then, surely, two-to-one is the magic ratio because I'm doing twice as many positive interactions as negative interactions.

Nope. Gottman says the magic ratio is five-to-one. Here's why.

Negative interactions carry more weight and have more impact on us. I've heard it said that negative interactions are like Velcro. They just stick to us. They're harder to let go. Positive interactions, unfortunately, are more like Teflon. They can kind of slide off. So, in order to tip the scales in your favor, Gottman discovered a five-to-one ratio leads to the most success in marriages and helps couples get past contempt.

But how does this magic ratio play out and work in your relationship on a daily basis? How do you even get started when you are stuck with this cloud of negativity or underappreciation hanging over your marriage? You have to start with small things. Small things can build up and become bigger things.

My wife and I have found our five positive interactions can be either verbal or nonverbal. It could be when you walk into the room, you simply smile at your spouse. That counts as a positive interaction. In today's technological world, it could be something as simple as sending a text or a goofy emoji. As you start with those small things, you'll find that once you get into the habit, you prime the pump. Then you've shifted things in your marriage. Instead of feeling a funk in your marriage, you feel refreshed.

I know you've heard you should never keep score in your marriage. In many ways, that's good advice. Gottman's ratio will be undone if I start to keep score on how many times my spouse has complimented me today, or in the past week. But it's good to keep score if I'm making a concerted effort to give my spouse five positive affirmations for every negative comment.

The more we complimented each other, the more positives we noticed. As Proverbs 11:25 says, "whoever refreshes others will be refreshed."

whoever
REFRESHES
others will be
refreshed.

PROVERBS 11:25, NIV

Draw it out:

1. What is one thing you respect and/or appreciate about your spouse? Share your answer with them now.

2. Prior to today, what do you think the ratio of positive to negative interactions has been in your marriage?

Pray together:

Thank God that you don't have to stay in the negative seasons of your marriage. If you find yourself in a funk where positive interactions seem lacking, ask His forgiveness for not appreciating the gift of your spouse. Seek the Lord's help in flooding your marriage with positive interactions. And to help you both live out Proverbs 11:25 by being refreshing to one another and allowing that to overflow into your family.

One Plank at a Time

By Carlos Santiago

> Now Adam knew Eve his wife, and she conceived and bore Cain...
>
> GENESIS 4:1

"I have to tell you something."

These words marked the beginning of a conversation I didn't want to have.

When I told my wife that day I was struggling with pornography, her image of me was shattered. Even worse, she felt betrayed. In my mind, my problem had little to do with her. It wasn't until my sin was out in the open that I could see the impact it had. She lost confidence in herself and no longer believed I thought she was beautiful. She was able to forgive me, but we spent the next couple of years struggling to rebuild what had been lost.

The Bible uses the term "to know" when it refers to sex, not because it is scared to say the word, but because sex conveys so much more than a physical act, a way to experience pleasure or reproduce. Sex is designed as a renewal, reaffirmation, and celebration of the till-death-do-us-part covenant we made when we got married. Through marriage, we come "to know" our spouse in a deeper way than any other relationship on earth.

But what happens when one person is completely vulnerable, holding nothing back, and the other person is hiding something? Whether the secret is mental, emotional, physical, in the present, or in the past, the damage is similar.

It makes us look at the person next to us and think, *I thought I knew you, but I was wrong. What else are you hiding?*

The marriage journey is often like crossing a wooden suspension bridge. In the beginning, it feels a little wobbly, maybe a little scary, but you move forward confident it will hold strong. Then halfway across the chasm, one of the planks breaks under your feet and everything changes. Suddenly, you are paralyzed in fear: You're too far to turn back but possess no strength to move forward. Your brain tells you the path toward restoration in marriage starts with repentance and forgiveness, but how can you trust the next plank won't break too? No matter how sturdy they might appear, do you dare put your full weight on it? But trust must be rebuilt—step by step.

Rebuilding trust requires we understand that the testing at each step is not a punishment or evidence of unforgiveness. It's easy to resist and cry out, "How many times do I have to say I'm sorry!?" or "Why can't we put this behind us?" But the process can't be rushed. If you are trying to rebuild trust, accept this testing as a sign of your spouse's desire to keep moving forward. Let your spouse test the next board. If you're struggling in the way I did, share where you are going, the password to your phone, and your browsing history. Do whatever it takes to prove the next plank won't break.

Jesus can free us from the entanglement of our sin (that's luo). But when we invite our spouse into the process, it becomes easier to not get tangled again. Over time, the transparency will allow trust to be rebuilt and the real you to be known.

A few years after that initial conversation, my wife and I were on a hike and passed a tree uprooted in a storm. As we looked at the tree, we couldn't help but see it as a symbol of our marriage. We stood in silence for a while, just staring at it. Then my wife noticed new growth coming out of the root ball, reaching upwards. The tree had been knocked over, but it was refusing to die. After a moment, she turned to me and gave me a curious look, studying my face as if seeing me for the first time. Then, with an almost surprised tone, she said, "I love you."

She'd said those words a thousand times before, but this time it was different. This time, she knew my struggles, my shame, and my failures. She knew every twisted and broken part of me, yet, she was deciding to love me anyway. She repeated the words over and over, "I love you. I love you. I love you." Each time, building in excitement until she was almost giddy. At that moment, I experienced a love I had only experienced once before. It was a powerful, godly love like the love Jesus had offered me. And I realized what it meant to be known. And set free.

Draw it out:

1. Think of an area in your marriage where you're reluctant to share. Is it financial? Your thought life? Relationships? Something from your past?

2. What would it look like if you were to invite your spouse into that sin? How might they help you untangle it?

3. If you're currently trying to rebuild trust, what steps can you take to prove "the next plank" won't break?

Pray together:

Ask God to reveal areas of your life you are prone to hide from your spouse. Ask for the grace needed to offer forgiveness and/or the courage needed to seek it. Thank God for your spouse and the help they can offer in untangling your sins, helping you grow more Christ-like together.

YADA

Much like the English use of "know," yada possesses a wide spectrum: simply, as knowing the route to the grocery store and, intimately, as an alternate term for sexual intercourse. This one verb carries both types of knowing: the cerebral/intellectual and the personal. Our emphasis here, however, is on the deeper, more intimate rendering.

When God "yadas" us, there is a flavor of protection and care to it: "For the LORD knows the way of the righteous" (Psalm 1:6). When we yada God, it implies a fierce bond: "Make me to know your ways . . ." (Psalm 25:4). In marriage, yada is the epitome of intimacy. The knowledge you possess of your spouse, cultivated by time, experience, and covenant, is nothing less than glorious.

The Masterful Metaphor

By Ron Deal

> *Then God said, "Let us make man in our image, after our likeness."*

GENESIS 1:26

I'm a metaphor-lover. I've happily crafted metaphors using everything from shopping carts to Crockpots. Metaphors are like Polaroids: instant pictures to help someone visualize a thousand words, so to speak.

But it's clear from the Bible I'm not the only one. God's a metaphor-lover. I mean, I'm pretty proud of the Crockpot idea, but He employs visuals so much more tactile and Technicolor.

So take a minute with me to imagine, hopefully not heretically, that you're the Trinity, before the world's been created. You're immaterial and eternal. John 4:24 tells us, "God is spirit," right? But you're going to create humankind—flesh and blood, who can't fully understand you.

So in God's genius, the Trinity creates in human beings all the elements of who the Trinity is so that They can reveal themselves. It's as if God was into photography long before photography was a thing. Genesis 1:26 says, "Let us make man in our image, after our likeness." In that likeness—that 3-D, experiential, Polaroid likeness—the Trinity will teach us about who They are and how to have a relationship with Them. At the same time, They'll show us more of who we are, how our nature is created—and how we function best.

(Theological caveat here: The Trinity is always the original concept here. The Trinity is not the Polaroid. If we get those confused, using earthly relationships like marriage as our "original" to understand God, we're remaking God in *our* image—which Exodus 20:4 forbids us to do in the Ten Commandments.)

To further their revelation, the Trinity creates symbols in the way we interact with one another as humans, even within very intimate relationships, like marriage, parenting, sexuality. Some theologians have said the Trinity is a communion of love and oneness, so They wired into us the ability to recreate oneness—and in so doing, see God more clearly.

When you stop and you think about it, it's brilliant.

In unified community, we can see the Godhead. Because the Trinity is seamless, breathtaking community. "The Lord our God, the Lord is one," says Deuteronomy 6:4, and then proceeds to tell us to communicate His oneness and our complete love for Him to the next generation through our parenting. The closer our relationships replicate who God is, the more we can come to know who our triune God is and how to live in relationship with Him. "Behold, how good and pleasant it is when brothers dwell in unity!" (Psalm 133:1).

The intimacy of marriage forms the perfect frame for God's metaphor of who He is. We experience commitment and faithfulness, separate, yet, together. And then, in sex, that oneness is ramped up; there's surrender and uniting in a way that's indescribable, even ecstatic. And it's built right into our physiology and bodily desires.

But wait! Isn't that only two people? Isn't the Trinity "God in three persons"? That's where procreation comes into play. Every child born creates a trinity of persons; a family whose love for one another glimpses the Original.

But because of sin, our relationships tend toward fracture and selfishness rather than unity and love. We constantly need to go back to the Original and strive to live out of our likeness.

Compared to most ways of planet earth, God's kingdom is upside down. The first will be last (Matthew 19:30). We lose our life to find it (Matthew 10:39). And we die to self to be able to give and love and sacrifice for the beloved (Romans 6:1-14).

A unified God is our original, and that's the way our relationships best operate. To pursue oneness as a couple, we have to surrender to who God calls us to be, aligning ourselves and our marriages in detail to who God is, as our "original."

This does mean dying to yourself in order to find it; channeling your power and all resources available to you, giving them away to empower others; surrendering your "rights" and even yourself into who God calls you to be. That's when you not only discover the best, most vibrant, fully functioning self and love your wife or child or neighbor as yourself. You also build a family rooted in God's own nature, and reflect His love out into the world in a masterful metaphor.

Draw it out:

1. In what ways have you glimpsed God's character through your own marriage?

2. Tell your spouse about a time when you understood more about God through your relationship.

3. How has your marriage changed you for the better, to be more like God?

Pray together:

Thank God for His stunning metaphor of marriage—for the ways you see and know and can even represent Him through this "profound mystery" (Ephesians 5:32). In the everyday, ask Him to show you ways your metaphor doesn't match who He is. Ask Him to increase your desire to experience His character and oneness in your marriage.

Sex Is Like Legos

By Dr. Juli Slattery

> *Set me as a seal upon your heart,*
> *as a seal upon your arm,*
> *for love is strong as death,*
> *jealousy is fierce as the grave.*
> *Its flashes are flashes of fire,*
> *the very flame of the LORD.*

SONG OF SOLOMON 8:6

Because I raised three sons, I know a thing or two about Legos. And here's one: It helps to know what you are building.

Think of your sex life as a "building project," like Legos. What are you and your spouse supposed to be building? Many couples feel lost as they try to make sense of pieces that don't seem to fit together and cause more frustration than joy.

After twenty-eight years of marriage, I can relate. My husband's and my relationship didn't check some of the common boxes of "sexual brokenness": no addiction, no trauma. But as I narrowed my focus as a clinical psychologist toward godly, authentic intimacy, I began to realize how lost we felt in navigating sexual intimacy in our marriage. In fact, there were times we operated from the wrong understanding of what a healthy, Christian sex life should even look like.

As I've interacted with thousands of couples over the years, I've found it's common to be building from a foundation of subtle lies that make the foundation of your sex life feel confusing and unstable. Lies like, "All your sexual desires will be met in marriage."

Our culture fuels this belief, for example, through pornography, which teaches you to be a sexual consumer. Porn (and even romance movies!) teaches you that people are there for you to objectify, use, and meet your needs. You don't have to be patient or loving during sex. You don't have to practice any self-denial.

Without realizing it, you could transpose our culture's lie onto your spouse: "God gave me this man or woman to meet all my sexual needs." Then when your spouse is difficult to love, or married sex doesn't meet your every fantasy, you feel cheated.

But sex was created by God as a celebration of covenant love. It's not about getting a demand or desire met through forcing or manipulating your spouse. What you are really supposed to build with those Legos is love! God is far more concerned about your love life than your sex life. Those challenges and disappointments you encounter are actually invitations to learn to love like God loves.

Another common lie is that sex primarily exists for the husband's pleasure. For wives, this quickly transforms sex into a duty to meet their husband's needs.

For the first decade of my marriage, I believed God wanted me to endure the physical pain I experienced during sex, to keep my husband from being tempted outside our marriage. Like cleaning the bathroom, I'd think, *It's been three days. Better do it again.*

I now understand God created sex as a celebration of committed, passionate, faithful unity. And whatever gets in the way, be it physical pain or emotional trauma or conflict, God wants us to address those so we can enter into the full gift of what He designed.

Another popular lie: God is only concerned about whether or not we're obeying the rules of sexual morality. *Is this particular act a sin?* It's an important question! But there's so much more to your sex life than keeping rules. See, God's also concerned about our sexual maturity. Long after you tie the knot, He's working on our character through sex, building something that can take your breath away in more ways than one.

Let me put it this way. When I was struggling with seeing sex as a duty in that first decade of marriage, I was picking up Legos in my boys' playroom. And it was as if God said to me, "Juli, think about sex more like a gift of Legos."

With Legos, you don't get the completed project you see on the front of the box, the cool castle or the car. You get mysterious pieces of plastic. You have to learn to build, to create something beautiful—which can be reshaped into something else in a different season.

You build Legos to represent a model of something in real life (a car, a castle, a town). In the Bible, sexual intimacy is presented as a model of the way God loves His people. You are called to be building that kind of love as you interact sexually within marriage!

Let's make that practical. Here are four specific ways God loves His people. Notice how these four "pillars" of God's love also show up in a healthy sex life:

1. **Faithfulness.** God is true to His character and His promises, to the point of being jealous for us. God similarly calls you to be true to and sexually exclusive with your spouse.

2. **Intimate knowing.** Your relationship with God isn't static. It's designed to grow in intimacy. In marriage, you should know each other more intimately today than you did a year ago, and sex is a big part of that journey.

3. **Sacrificial love.** God's ultimate demonstration of covenant love for us is Jesus' death on the cross. In fact, you can't love without sacrifice. So why are we surprised when the expression of covenant love and sexuality also requires self-denial and sacrifice?

4. **Passionate celebration.** Christians are encouraged to gather regularly to connect and celebrate our love for God through worship. In a similar way, a husband and wife are encouraged to be together regularly to celebrate with their bodies the covenant they have with one another.

As with any Lego creation, if you have three of these pillars but not all four, your sex life will be imbalanced. While no marriage will ever reach perfection in modeling God's love, we can all be building toward the fullness of God's design for sex.

Draw it out:

1. Name one lie you've personally believed about sex.

2. Which of Dr. Slattery's four pillars have you experienced most in your sexual relationship? How does it help you understand God more deeply?

3. Which might be the weakest pillar of your sexual relationship? What's one practical step you can take this month to intentionally build that pillar?

Pray together:

Even if you struggle to see it right now, express your personal gratitude for and trust in God's wisdom and goodness in giving your marriage the gift of sex. But rather than getting caught up in what your sexual relationship should be, remember that sex—and our relationship with God—is "naked and unashamed" (Genesis 2:25). So along with gratitude, approach God with honesty about what your sex life is and isn't. Ask Him to help you, individually and together, love more like He loves His people.

GOD created *sex* as a celebration of

committed,

passionate,

faithful

unity.

What Are Your Sexpectations?

By Brian Goins

Finally, brothers, whatever is true, whatever is honorable, whatever is just, whatever is pure, whatever is lovely, whatever is commendable, if there is any excellence, if there is anything worthy of praise, think about these things.

PHILIPPIANS 4:8

When did you first start developing sexpectations, or sexual expectations?

Some of our sexpectations are formed by our culture: friends, TV shows, etc. (For me, it was that iconic scene from Top Gun [the original] where Tom Cruise serenades Kelly McGillis. All I needed was a bomber jacket, cheesy love song, and charming smile, and the ladies would love me.) Some are just the result of the natural differences in marriage— shaped by gender, family background, childhood experiences, personality differences, and much more.

I've found that in marriage, it's easier to have unspoken sexual expectations rather than real conversations. I expect my wife, Jen, to read my mind, to intuitively know when I'm in the mood, what I want her to wear (or not wear), and how she should "surprise" me with a clandestine rendezvous.

Of course, Jen has her own set of sexpectations. I would ask her, but I'm concerned they would differ too greatly from mine! But I've been married long enough to know they involve touching her heart before I touch her body, making sure the kids are in the fifth stage of REM sleep, and triple-locking the doors before we enjoy intimacy.

Unfortunately, when our sexpectations don't meet reality, what's left is often frustration, disappointment, and isolation. Two becoming one devolves into two becoming . . . none.

I'm fairly certain God wants us to have great sex. After all, He invented it. (And let's just go on record saying that was a far better invention than the microchip.) Out of sixty-six books in the Bible, He devoted a whole book just to the topic of sex (Song of Solomon). And just after He created Adam and Eve, He turned on some Marvin Gaye music and told them to "get it on."

Okay, Marvin Gaye may be a stretch, but I'm pretty sure scholars will tell you that "get it on" in Hebrew is translated "naked and unashamed."

Scripture says enough about sex in marriage that I can point to at least three sexpectations God had when He created intimacy between a man and a woman:

- **Procreation** (Genesis 1:28). Although in a fallen world, not everyone has the privilege to procreate.

- **Recreation** (Song of Solomon). The Bible encourages those who are married to enjoy each other's bodies.

- **Proclamation** (Ephesians 5:31-32). When two spouses become one flesh, they paint a physical picture of a spiritual reality.

Sex is a powerful experience in marriage, but I find it's easy to allow unrealistic or even harmful expectations to run rampant through my mind and ruin our intimacy. When that happens, I need to stop and ask a few questions:

1. What's fueling them?

Whether we fuel our sexpectations from TV shows, films, porn, or erotic novels, fantasy has an uncanny ability to sabotage our reality.

This is why Job made a covenant with his eyes—not to let what he sees mess with what he has (Job 31:1). This is why Paul says, "Whatever is true, whatever is honorable, whatever is just, whatever is pure, whatever is lovely, whatever is commendable, if there is any excellence, if there is anything worthy of praise, think about these things" (Philippians 4:8).

2. Am I thinking about my spouse's sexual expectations more than my own?

Sexually speaking, we should think far more about our spouse's expectations than our own (Philippians 2:3). Christ told His disciples that when we die to self we actually find life. Perhaps if we died to our own unrealistic sexual expectations, we might renew our sex life as well.

3. When was the last time we had a real conversation about intimacy?

The word intercourse actually means, "interpersonal communication." Every couple should make time to have some intercourse about intercourse. Ask your spouse how he or she would rate your sex life. What would make it better? Is there anything you could do to help create more satisfying intimacy?

Solomon wasted many years chasing his sexpectations. Toward the end of his days, he passed some advice onto his son: "Rejoice in the wife of your youth, a lovely deer, a

Rejoice

in the wife of your

YOUTH.

PROVERBS 5:18

graceful doe, let her breasts fill you at all times with delight; be intoxicated always in her love" (Proverbs 5:18-19).

If you find your expectations about sex are leaving you frustrated, ask yourself what is fueling them, match them to God's expectations, and try having a real conversation about them with your spouse.

No bomber jacket or cheesy love song required . . . unless you want it to be.

Draw it out:

1. What expectations for intimacy did you have coming into marriage? How do these conflict or agree with your spouse's?

2. How does your spouse define "intimacy"? If you don't know, ask each other. It's about time you had that conversation.

Pray together:

Thank God for the gift of intimacy with your spouse. Ask for Him to make you aware of any unspoken—or even unhealthy—expectations you may have. If needed, confess any ways you have taken your spouse and your marriage for granted in this area. Pray for your marriage bed to be blessed, that the two of you may truly become one in intimacy.

Draw closer:

When it comes to marital sex . . . what's normal? Host Brian Goins and researcher Shaunti Feldhahn dive into all your questions about married life and the bedroom in Married with Benefits™. Listen to the conversation at FamilyLife.com/DrawnTogetherBonus.

Whatever is

TRUE,

Whatever is

HONORABLE,

Whatever is

JUST,

Whatever is

PURE,

Whatever is

LOVELY,

Whatever is

COMMENDABLE,

if there is any excellence,

if there is anything worth of praise,

think about these things.

PHILIPPIANS 4:8

What We Wish Someone Would Have Told Us about Sex

By Dave and Ann Wilson

> *Let your fountain be blessed,*
> *and rejoice in the wife of your youth . . .*

PROVERBS 5:18

We went to FamilyLife's Weekend to Remember marriage getaway two weeks before our wedding—didn't really listen. "We don't need this stuff. All those other couples are struggling because they're not as in love with each other as we are."

We thought marriage was going to be amazing because we loved Jesus, and we were in love.

I (Ann) had a whole picture of what Dave was going to be like. I thought he was going to lead our family spiritually. He was going to hug me and kiss me every day. Dave thought we'd have sex multiple times a day, and I'd be chasing him around the house. Both of us thought sex was going to be amazing and the easiest part of our marriage.

We were so naïve to think it would be easy. When you crawl in bed with your spouse, you're not just bringing two bodies. You're bringing all your history, all your thoughts and beliefs and even teachings you've heard about sex. And it gets complicated.

We didn't realize all the baggage we carried in our pre-married life was going to come with us into marriage. You think, "That's in the past. It's done. It's over." You don't realize it's coming with you, and marriage will be the relationship that brings it out. Stuff we thought was buried and gone was just waiting to erupt.

Sexual abuse was one larger piece of baggage I (Ann) brought in. I thought it was in the past. But when we got married and Dave would touch me, I was so reactive. I continually pushed him away. I didn't know what love and physical intimacy looked like apart from abuse.

A lot of my (Dave) sexual brokenness came from my struggle with pornography. It was my little secret. I didn't tell the guys I was meeting for accountability with; I didn't tell Ann. Until I realized this secret was destroying my walk with God and destroying my marriage.

It was easier for me to talk about sex as a pastor. A husband and wife making love is something good in God's eyes. I can teach that. But when I walked into our home and needed to talk about my sexual relationship with Ann—things I was disappointed in, things she was disappointed in, things I needed to learn—I didn't want to talk about that. That's scary.

Talking about sex is scary because it's intimate. Very intimate. We're afraid to talk about it because we just assume that we're failing, or we think the other person is disappointed in every way. But we've got to talk about it.

One thing a couple can do is to say, "Hey, let's just talk about how we're doing in this area." But always start by praying about that conversation. It's so sensitive. Pray that God will allow you to say things that are honest, yet loving and kind. Because the way we talk about this makes a difference.

We both also had to learn to understand each other's view of sexual intimacy. I (Dave) wrongly thought, *Let's get naked, let's make love, that's sex.*

Sex to Ann was so much deeper and more intimate. Ann wanted affection. Nonsexual touch. Conversation and communication. To her, that was all part of sex. Then I realized she does want to have sex; she just approaches it differently.

We also had to learn what true intimacy is. Not just physical intimacy, but every form of intimacy—emotionally, spiritually, and physically. How do those aspects come together? Because we never knew they did. A lot of us were taught that sex is wrong; it's dirty. But sex in marriage really is soul bonding. When you make love, it's deeper than just two bodies. It's soul to soul. And God celebrates that in a marriage.

Once we understood that, it helped us to become better lovers, not just physical lovers. We learned to love each other as we each longed to be loved, and that impacted our sexual relationship as well.

Draw it out:

1. What beliefs, thoughts, and teachings about sex did you bring into marriage?

2. What's one thing you wish someone would have told you about married sex?

3. Remembering to be loving and kind—what's one thing you long for your spouse to know that could make your sex life more fulfilling?

Pray together:

Thank God for the gift of sex in a marriage, for His unique design in bringing a husband and wife together in mind, body, and soul. Ask His forgiveness for any ways you have not treated your sexual relationship with your spouse as a gift, and ask for His help in creating a healthy, loving relationship in your marriage.

What You Really Long For

By Carlos Santiago

And the man and his wife were both naked and were not ashamed.

GENESIS 2:25

I made a quick trip to the supermarket to find some firewood, hoping it would help set the mood for a romantic evening. At the checkout, I couldn't help but notice every magazine seemed to know what I was up to. They all offered "amazing advice" to spice things up in the bedroom. As enticing as the titles were, I've been married long enough to know that advice from grocery store magazines won't do much good. When sex becomes infrequent, unenthusiastic, and disappointing, the answers are found much closer to home.

As a counselor, I'm often asked by one spouse how they can get the other to be more interested in sex. I'll ask, "If you could get your spouse to agree to have sex with you as often as you'd like for the rest of your married life, but you would never talk to each other again, would you want that?" No one ever says yes. Why? Because sex was designed to be more than just a mindless physical act. We want it to bring connection. We want to feel loved, desired, respected, known, and understood. We think sex will bring us that. But the frequency and quality of sex we complain about is really the outward sign of an unmet inward need. What we long for is intimacy.

Sex is a deeply intimate act, but it doesn't *create* intimacy; it expresses it. Slapping on a new "technique" or special outfit to a relationship devoid of intimacy might offer temporary pleasure, but it will ultimately leave us feeling hollow as if we're putting on a show. It's no wonder society talks of sexual performance issues. Sex without intimacy is just that—a performance.

Unfortunately, for many of us, that's what sex has become. We live in the same house but live separate lives. We feel like strangers, and we try to "fake it till we make it." But, as busy as we typically are, we can't place all the blame on our work schedules or the kids. Sometimes, the distance we feel is the direct result of our own actions.

I've been there. Early in our marriage, I spent all day at work solving other people's problems. When I'd come home, my wife would try and tell me about a situation she had dealt with that day. But before she would finish, I'd cut her off and start giving her a solution. I thought I was being helpful. I wanted to ease her discomfort as quickly as possible. Unfortunately, what I was really doing was telling her that her problems were simple, and her feelings were an overreaction. I made her feel stupid and, over time, taught her to keep her struggles to herself.

Sometimes, I've discovered, my spouse doesn't need an answer. Sometimes, she can't explain the way she feels. Sometimes, she just needs my understanding or, at the very least, my presence. If she suspects that she'll have to justify her feelings or that her complex problem will be disrespected with a quick answer, she may learn to keep it to herself, or worse, find someone else to talk to.

And all this was with me trying to be helpful. Imagine the damage that can be done when any of us intentionally belittles a spouse. Fights for many couples follow a pattern of perpetual escalation, each attempting to outdo the other with insults in a marital nuclear arms race. After the dust settles, the fallout lingers.

For other couples, the insults are more subtle and strategic. A sigh, roll of the eyes, or a condescending comment under the breath are all that is needed to get your way. But whether the disrespect comes from a direct attack, is muttered under your breath, or is communicated completely unintentionally, the results are the same. Disrespect shuts down intimacy. It's hard to be "in the mood" when you don't feel respected.

Genesis 2:25 describes the initial, sinless relationship between Adam and Eve by saying, "the man and his wife were both naked and were not ashamed." Beyond the obvious physical application, "naked and not ashamed" also means knowing you can share what's going on inside your heart without fear of rejection. It means knowing that, even when you are at your worst, you're still loved.

If you can share that type of intimacy, it won't matter if you look amazing naked, what music is playing, or if you got the fireplace just right. You'll be comfortable in your own skin. You'll be free to explore, linger, and experiment with different ways of expressing your love for your spouse. Sometimes that means you'll experience mind-blowing orgasms. Other times, you might feel more of a fizzle. But it won't matter either way. When you have real intimacy, you'll have what you really long for.

Draw it out:

1. What is your natural posture when your spouse shares an opinion? Is your first reaction to try to understand or argue a different perspective?

2. Have you ever shied away from specific topics for fear of your spouse's reaction?

3. What do you think is a barrier to greater intimacy (and maybe a better sex life) in your marriage?

Pray together:

Thank God for the gift of your spouse and the intimacy He created for the two of you to share. Ask Him to show you how you can listen better to what is on their heart, to create an atmosphere of being "naked and not ashamed." Ask God to help you find the words to increase your communication and establish greater intimacy in your marriage.

The Silent Killer in Your Marriage

By D.A. Horton

> *Instead, speaking the truth in love, we will grow to become in every respect the mature body of him who is the head, that is, Christ.*

EPHESIANS 4:15 (NIV)

I've spent years lying to and robbing my wife.

You see, I've struggled with this since I was a little boy, and, unfortunately, this carried over into my marriage. But I never realized I was lying to my wife. The lies are typically very subtle, and I always seem to have a good reason or something used to justify my lying.

Here's how these conversations go. My wife, Elicia, will ask me a simple question like, "What's wrong?" Keep in mind, my wife and I have been friends since we were kids. She knows me better than anyone. She knows me well enough to discern when something is wrong. (By now, you've probably guessed my response . . . probably because you've responded in a similar way.)

My response is typically, "Nothing" or "I'm good." But I'm lying. Usually, there is so much wrong in that moment. While this lying may be subtle and seemingly insignificant, what I said is not the truth.

Honesty in that moment looks like sharing the truth, even if that means gently telling her, "I'm offended by what you said/did." Or when I'm dealing with things that leave me feeling insecure, I can get really vulnerable and let her know, "I don't feel like you find me attractive," or "I'm not sure I'm capable of handling this or that."

Most often, instead, I resort to my behavior pattern developed over 40 years: I don't tell her the truth, and I shut down emotionally and conversationally.

Have you been there? It seems insignificant—even when I think I have a "good" reason—but it can be a silent killer in your marriage.

Here's what happens when I do this. I exclude my wife from experiencing—from fully knowing—all of me. Which also excludes her from parts of our marriage. I'm wrong for that.

When I withhold the truth from Elicia, or share it with someone else, it's like robbing her. She deserves the truth in my heart; she needs it. Without it, she and I won't experience the loving kindness and the deeper intimacy God has for us in marriage.

My reasons for doing this come from believing a lie that love and disappointment can't coexist in a healthy marriage. But I'm wrong. Love and disappointment do coexist in marriage. And when they do, that tension reflects the steadfast and covenant love God has for us. The same love that was deposited into our hearts when we accepted His gift of salvation. What an amazing gift it is and what amazing breakthroughs come as a result of its presence in our marriage.

This revelation has given Elicia and me so much freedom, growth, and maturity in our marriage. The Apostle Paul gives us an amazing picture of this in Ephesians 4:15 when he says, "Instead, speaking the truth in love, we will grow to become in every respect the mature body of Him who is the head, that is, Christ."

The opposite of that says we will lack growth, we will lack maturity, and we will not grow in Christ. Which means to me, no matter the situation, sharing the truth of my heart, in love and as fits the occasion (Ephesians 4:15, 29), must happen—remaining conscious of not just what I want to say, but where my wife is at, too.

Who else is deserving of that from my heart?

SPEAK
the truth in
love.

Draw it out:

1. Write down some of the thoughts, feelings, disappointments, or insecurities you've not shared with your spouse.

2. What has kept you from sharing the truth with your spouse when it comes to the things you listed above?

3. Pray with your spouse and have an honest conversation about one of the things you've listed above.

Pray together:

Thank God for His steadfast love and for depositing His love in your hearts. Thank Him for the ability to love one another even when disappointed in each other. Ask Him to help you create new habits of honest and open conversations that result in growth as a couple, maturity in marriage, and growth in Christ.

I See You

By Leslie J. Barner

*Two are better than one, because they have a good
reward for their toil. For if they fall, one will lift up his
fellow. But woe to him who is alone when he falls and
has not another to lift him up!*

ECCLESIASTES 4:9-10

After a long battle with heart disease, medicine was no longer
helping to give my husband, Aubrey, quality of life. His heart
was failing, and we were running out of options.

During an extended hospital stay, his cardiology team
told us he would need an electronic device implanted into
his chest to help his heart pump efficiently until he could get
a new heart. Without this open-heart surgery, he'd only have
about six months to live. This option sounded promising, but
the list of possible complications and the reality of our future
new normal were so overwhelming, *my* heart sank.

I don't think I have ever been more afraid in my life. But I
desperately wanted to be strong and courageous for Aubrey
and our family. So I carefully hid my feelings.

I spent a lot of time in prayer, seeking God's comfort,
peace, and strength. In His grace, He held me together day
after day. Yet I longed for human connection—someone in
close proximity to talk to about my feelings, concerns, and all
we were facing. But we had no other family in the state where
we had relocated with my husband's job. There were days I felt
alone and unseen.

Then one day, while walking the halls of the hospital, one of Aubrey's doctors hurried toward me. "Mrs. Barner!" he shouted. "I've been looking all over for you!" My mind raced. What could be so important that he would track me down? He went on to tell me Aubrey had shared with him that I had some fears and concerns about the surgery.

"What?" I responded in shock. "I never told him that."
The doctor spent several minutes compassionately addressing my concerns. He answered every question and helped calm my fears. After our conversation, I felt settled and at peace.

As the doctor and I parted ways, I realized Aubrey had seen beyond the façade I'd been putting on. I was immediately reminded of a scene from the 2009 movie, *Avatar*. In a heartwarming scene, Neytiri—feeling as if she had come to know Jake intimately—put her hand over his heart and said, "I *see* you." In her world, this phrase was better understood, "I see into you" or "I understand you."

Aubrey asking his doctor to talk with me was his way of saying, "I *see* you." In that moment, I felt seen, heard, fully known, and deeply loved. For me, it was a beautiful picture of Mark 10:8: "'. . . and the two shall become one flesh.' So they are no longer two but one flesh."

But what does it really mean to be "one flesh"? According to God's design for marriage, this is two people, husband and wife, coming together into a covenant relationship and connecting in a deeply intimate and beautiful way—body and soul. And while this includes sexual intimacy, it doesn't begin with the body; this deep connection begins with the heart.

Experiencing this level of "one flesh-ness" or intimacy requires humility, openness, transparency, and trust. It requires loving each other unconditionally, in our nakedness (our authentic, imperfect selves) without judgment, and yet speaking the truth in love to address conflict and sin. That level of closeness requires forgiveness, showing up for each other, being each other's best ally, and being an unbeatable team against all odds.

I once heard someone say that to truly become one flesh, you have to commit to a lifetime of learning about your spouse—to truly know them. I've noticed some true things about good students:

1. They pay attention.

2. They make learning a priority.

3. They take good notes.

4. They put into practice what they've learned.

If you were given a test on how well you know your spouse today, what grade would you receive? Whether your knowledge of your spouse might fall above or below average, consider putting those four truths about good students into practice and watch your relationship grow as you begin (or continue) to move toward each other in a deep and beautiful way—like Aubrey moved toward me.

TWO are *better* than ONE.

Draw it out:

1. What's one area where you feel intimately known or understood by your spouse? What's one way you long for them to know you more? Without judgment, share with each other how you feel.

2. One idea to be a better student of your spouse: regularly connect over meaningful conversation. It's during these times that you can discover more about each other's personalities, preferences, favorites, concerns, fears, hopes, dreams. Here are a few conversation starters to give it a go!

- As a kid, what was one of your dreams for the future?

- Tell me something I don't know about you.

- If you were planning an amazing day, what activities would be in the plan?

- When was the last time you had a good belly laugh?

- What's one of your biggest fears or concerns?

Pray together:

Thank God for giving you each other to experience the gift of "oneness." Ask Him to help you be faithful in your commitment to a lifetime of learning about each other so that it moves you both toward being fully known and deeply loved. Pray that in the process of learning, loving, and growing closer together, your marriage will impact and encourage other couples and future generations for His glory.

What the NFL Didn't Teach Me about Sex

By Derwin and Vicki Gray

I praise you, for I am fearfully and wonderfully made.
Wonderful are your works; my soul knows it very well.

PSALM 139:14

Since I (Derwin) was thirteen, football has been one of the most important things in my life. At that age, I decided football was going to provide a way out of my living situation and provide a better life. I dedicated years of my life to football, and it paid off with being drafted by the Indianapolis Colts in 1993, playing six years of professional football.

I learned a lot from my NFL days, and I even became a Christian thanks to one of my Colts teammates who shared Jesus with me. My life was changed for the better in many ways by football and the NFL. But one thing the NFL didn't teach me was about sex. More specifically, what "sexy" means to my wife, Vicki.

Coming out of college, I was a well-chiseled machine. I was five foot eleven and weighed a lean 200 pounds. Did I say I was lean? I had those coveted washboard abs all men desire. Forget a six pack, I had an eight pack. I was the epitome of "sexy," right? I just knew I was "that" guy, and I thought Vicki knew it too. Maybe she did, but it wasn't for the exact reasons I thought.

Even if I wasn't an NFL player, our situation and perspective on things when it comes to being sexy, attractive, and intimate with our spouses is similar to a lot of couples. In those early years of marriage, we love everything about each other, especially our bodies. Many of us are probably in the best physical shape of our lives, and this physical attraction is typically the first point of attraction.

I thought my lean, mean, football-playing body was the reason Vicki found me sexy. I was shocked when I learned that wasn't the biggest reason she was attracted to me or what led to physical intimacy. I learned one of the sexiest things to her I could do was wash the dishes. Yes, the dishes. I learned it was sexy to do the laundry. I learned it was sexy to vacuum. Chasing down a 200-pound man running forty yards in less than five seconds takes a lot more effort than doing the dishes, the laundry, or vacuuming. But those things mean so much more to my wife. That was a revelation!

After I learned that, I began celebrating things like vacuuming and making it known to Vicki. "I'm vacuuming baby, what's up?" Seriously, I learned physical intimacy doesn't only have to do with the physical aspect of things. It's her seeing and feeling, "Oh, you care about me and the things that I care about. You're partnering with me. You are doing things that take a load off of me." It's also learning how to love her, how to encourage her, how to be with her.

Let me (Vicki) chime in here. This is extremely important in year one, but probably more important in the later years of your marriage. We are thirty years in. Our bodies are not in the same physical condition, and Derwin can no longer chase down a grown man running a 4.5-second, forty-yard dash. There are more flabs than abs. Things have changed. We have changed, and love calls us to change with our spouse.

Wonderful
are your
WORKS.

PSALM 139:14

I find amazing beauty in that. This is the reason it's so important to touch the heart before attempting to take off the clothes. This applies to year one in marriage, as well as year thirty. And that's actually part of the fun in marriage. This gives you more opportunities to let your love grow deeper in more areas—beyond physicality. In these later years of marriage, emotional, intellectual, and spiritual intimacy are much more important. And you truly become one in Christ.

And let me tell you something. It gets better at every single level, but what makes it better is a Christ-centered focus and the Holy Spirit's presence. What a great place to be in your marriage! And as my husband said, it's something you won't learn from the NFL or whatever your focus is. But it is something that will last a lifetime and create an intimate, loving marriage.

Draw it out:

1. What do you think makes you sexy to your spouse?

2. What makes your spouse sexy to you?

3. Discuss the "whys" behind what you shared in the above questions.

Pray together:

Thank God for making you both "fearfully and wonderfully" made. Thank Him for creating levels of intimacy that aren't limited to just the physical. Ask for His help in learning the ways you can love your spouse better and in seeing all the wonderful ways He created them. Ask that your marriage would be an act of worship and give Him glory.

What Could Your Sex Life Become?

By Dr. Juli Slattery

> *Every good gift and every perfect gift is from above, coming down from the Father of lights, with whom there is no variation or shadow due to change.*

JAMES 1:17

You know how, as an adult, you can look back and see how your parents were really strong in some areas and really kind of bad in some others? In fact, maybe their greatest strength is their greatest weakness.

That parent who pulled out all the stops to do the fun stuff perhaps didn't teach you as well to be content with small, everyday happiness or maybe to save money. Or maybe your parents were great at teaching you to obey authority, but not to think for yourself in critical moments. I'm sure my sons would be happy to fill you in on the flip side of my "strengths."

In all honesty, the church has been guilty of the same thing. One of the ways I see an unbalanced approach in the church's past is the emphasis on "purity culture" of the 1990s and early 2000s. Though God created sex to be multifaceted, as the church, we emphasized only one aspect of sexuality: that sex is to be reserved for marriage.

In that rather narrow focus—like any parent in their strength—we've missed the fuller picture of God's design for sex as the physical celebration of the covenant promise of marriage. Yes, when you have sex outside of that covenant promise you lack integrity. However, in purity culture, the church only emphasized sexual morality—keeping rules—not integrity or sexual wholeness. Because of that, a lot of couples feel stuck. They may know what not to do, but they have no roadmap to wholeness.

Many Christian couples do not know how to explore and enjoy sexuality because all they know are the rules. They don't see the broader vision of why God says an emphatic "yes!" to sex.

Maybe you told yourself "no" sexually for a lot of years—and that you should repress all sexual desire, all sexual thought. But now that you're married, perhaps it's tough to delight in God's creation of you as a sexual person. You may even feel shame in being sexual with your spouse.

But that's not God's design! All you need to do is look at the Song of Solomon to see that both Solomon and his bride were fully enjoying the gift of sex. Both were invested in sexual pleasure and thought about each other sexually. "His mouth is most sweet, and he is altogether desirable. This is my beloved and this is my friend" (verse 5:16). And God, who put a whole

Every *perfect* GIFT is from above...

JAMES 1:17

book about sex in the Bible, said their enjoyment was a great thing.

Purity culture may have also left you with a lingering sense that sexual sin can never be truly forgiven.

God's design for pleasure and fun in sex is not just for perfect people or perfect couples. Jesus died to set you free from the sin of your past and the bondage of temptation in your life today. If we confess our sins, the Bible is clear that God forgives our sins and cleanses us from all unrighteousness (I John 1:9). Many Christians continue to punish themselves for their sexual sin by avoiding or repressing pleasure in marriage. Friend, this is not what God wants for you.

Even after marriage, we're constantly moving toward a greater degree of sexual integrity, which means surrendering our sexuality to the fullness of God's design for His glory. Why would God give sex to a married couple and say, "Enjoy this!"? God created hormones and genitals and orgasms. They weren't Satan's idea. Satan has aimed to twist your sexual desire, but he didn't create your sexuality. So what is the beauty in God's design for sex?

Sex is a whole-bodied expression, remembering and symbolizing your exclusive covenant with your spouse.

Like the sacrament of communion, sex is something holy and physical we do to remember a spiritual truth. God has given the ecstasy of sex to physically express, cement, and remember the passionate beauty of giving ourselves in promise and sacrifice and faithfulness to each other.

So yes, there are some ways the church, in her strengths, may have been culturally lopsided in our understanding of sex. But just like when you became an adult, it's your choice to intentionally lean into the deficits of what you previously understood.

With a fuller perspective of God's creation of sex—what could your sex life become?

Draw it out:

1. Were you taught some unhealthy perspectives on sex?

2. In Scripture, God indicates both of your sexual journeys matter. If your spouse struggles with sexual shame, prayerfully (and privately) consider what God would have you do to intentionally build sexual safety and delight for your spouse: "He brought me to the banqueting house, and his banner over me was love" (Song of Solomon 2:4).

3. What are two tangible ways you could lean into the ecstasy of sex with your spouse in the next month? (Keeping in mind that building safety around intimacy may need to come first.)

Pray together:

Thank God for making us sexual on purpose and giving us this lifetime sacrament of ecstasy and private celebration. Ask Him to reveal the ways you're missing the mark on all He created sex to be. Pray that your marriage bed would be one of safety, intimacy, and celebration.

EUANGELION

Have you received any good news recently? In the first century, to receive a good report was to receive an euangelion. Broken down, "eu" means "good" and "aggello" (similar to "angel") means "to declare." To declare something that is good.

This is where we get the English word "gospel" ("god" + "spell" = good saying). Although both euangelion and gospel are general words, in Christianity they specifically refer to the person and work of Jesus. It's the good report we've received that there is salvation from sin and God's wrath in the atoning death of Christ. Christians disagree on many issues. But what binds them together is the euangelion, the gospel. And the heart of the gospel is Jesus.

So it is with marriage. There are two individuals in the Christian marriage, which means there are disagreements. But when the marriage itself is based on Jesus, it endures. Now that indeed is good news!

What Really Matters

By Crawford and Karen Loritts

*So God created man in his own image,
in the image of God he created him;
male and female he created them.*

GENESIS 1:27

I (Crawford) come from a long line of strong, healthy marriages. My mom and dad never sat us down and said, "This is what you need to do in a marriage," but I saw it firsthand. Witnessing the love and respect my parents had for each other, I always knew I wanted a marriage like that. Those were the expectations I had when I asked Karen to marry me.

I (Karen) was raised by a single mother. I didn't see a husband and wife interacting in my home, but I remember watching my Sunday school teachers, the Borns. I remember observing how well they loved and served each other. I remember the tenderness I witnessed between them, and I remember thinking they really acted as one unit in their marriage.

When I met Crawford's parents, again, I watched how two godly people interacted with one another. They weren't the same person, they were different and even disagreed, but when they came together to decide on an issue, they spoke with one voice. And since I didn't have role models in my own home, I was kind of nervous when Crawford asked me to marry him. So I took my cues for what to do in married life from them.

Today, we've been married for more than fifty years and have eleven grandchildren. Hopefully, they've observed a healthy example of married life through our marriage and those of their parents. God willing, each of them will one day stand before family and friends and make similar vows to the ones we did on our wedding day. And if asked, here are two things we'd tell them as they start their lives together.

1. Don't fear commitment.

Don't be afraid of giving yourself completely to the person God brings into your life. One of the habits we wished we would have started earlier in our marriage was making sure we set aside time to talk (just us) every day. There can be a lot of joy when you are allowed to be your full self with someone. We laugh a lot and try not to take ourselves too seriously. I hope our grandchildren and their spouses laugh and enjoy one another. That's worth celebrating.

Also, be committed and intentional in your relationship with Jesus. Make Him the focal point of your marriage and make walking with Him a natural rhythm of married life.

2. Your relationship can make a difference.

Karen has relatives that have been married for decades. Even though they aren't believers, they've looked at our relationship and said, "I want that, too."

Our marriage is not just about us. One day your own children and grandchildren will be watching how you interact as a couple. Or maybe it's a neighbor, relative, or kid from church. Marriage is bigger than just the two of you. Embracing that has helped us be more intentional with how we live together as a couple and how we raised our family.

We want them to see the

FOOTPRINTS OF GOD

in their *lives.*

The purpose of marriage is to tell the truth about God during your moment in history. So don't wall yourself off. We all need other couples around us—older couples guiding us and younger couples we can pour a little of what we're learning into. And we need friends to help us understand, "No, you're not the only ones struggling with this."

Our time and influence on earth are limited. All of us are going to be dead one day. That sounds terribly morbid, but it's true. But when we look at our lives through that perspective, we can ask ourselves, what really matters?

Trips to Disney World, summer vacations, ball games— that's wonderful stuff. We're thankful we have a lot of fond memories to look back on from raising our kids and enjoying our grandchildren. And we hope they create memories with their families. But we want more for them. We want them to see the footprints of God in their lives.

Whether or not you had a healthy marriage modeled growing up, your marriage is serving as an example to others. When you look at your marriage today, tomorrow, fifty years from now ... what really matters? What truth about God are the people you're influencing learning?

Draw it out:

1. Name one thing you hope others see when observing your marriage. If you're in a tough spot right now, that's okay. Maybe you hope others are witnessing resilience or forgiveness.

2. In ten years, what do you hope others will witness?

3. What is one piece of advice you would give to a couple on their wedding day?

Pray together:

Thank God for the role models you've had in marriage. If you don't feel you've had any positive ones, ask Him to send you an older couple you can learn from. Thank Him for both the highs and lows in your relationship—both growing and shaping you into a marriage that can impact others. And in everyday life, ask God to help you stay focused on the things that matter for eternity.

Marriage is a Battlefield

By Laura Way

Finally, be strong in the Lord and in the strength of his might. Put on the whole armor of God, that you may be able to stand against the schemes of the devil.

EPHESIANS 6:10-11

On any given day, without the Holy Spirit's help, I live for my own good and, frankly, I expect my husband to live for me also. The annoyance rising in me that he's still watching basketball instead of initiating bedtime for our girls can get my blood boiling and my defense up for the rest of the night—never mind that I'm annoyed because I don't want to get up either.

Perhaps this is why, of all the pictures used—a father teaching a child to walk, a mother hen gathering her chicks, a good shepherd leading His sheep to safety—I find the image of marriage to reflect Jesus and the church is the most perplexing of all God's metaphors for Himself.

In the Old Testament, the picture of Himself made a bit more sense to me—God is like a patient husband to an unfaithful wife (that's us). But the image Paul gives in Ephesians 5 is infinitely more hopeful. "Submit to one another out of reverence for Christ . . . Wives, submit yourselves to your own husbands as you do to the Lord. . . . Husbands, love your wives, just as Christ loved the church and gave himself up for her . . . This is a profound mystery—but I am talking about Christ and the church" (verses 21-32, NIV).

Yes, Jesus had to go to great lengths to make the church (us again) His very own. But in this image, rather than being continuously unfaithful, the church—Jesus' bride—loves, respects, and submits to him.

What changed between the Old and New Testaments? Why, after Jesus' life, death, and resurrection, are we given the encouragement of a bride that responds in faithfulness to her husband? Marriage was created from the beginning to be a reflection of unity and love in the midst of difference. A safe place for the bliss of oneness and of mission. What can give us hope to live this out?

Without the Holy Spirit working in and through us, the story marriage tells is usually one of two broken people, hurting each other over and over until they give up on unity, safety, and bliss altogether.

It's no accident that immediately after Paul's instructions to husbands and wives (and children and parents, slaves and masters), He tells us to put on the armor of God. Because it is so counterintuitive and countercultural to serve, submit, put someone else's interest above our own, and love someone unconditionally (especially when they don't deserve it), marriage is a spiritual battlefield. Jesus came to turn the kingdom of this world upside-down, friends. This is why, during the NBA playoffs, the Holy Spirit reminds me to lay down my scorecard of who's doing more.

The world wants us to believe one thing about love and marriage: Its purpose is to make us happy. Jesus models a better love. The love we were made for. A love that sacrifices time, treasure, energy, comfort, and sometimes even blood for the beloved. A love that can see past immediate satisfaction all the way to the end—where we stand before God knowing our marriage told a beautiful story. Not a perfect one, mind you. But one where ashes were turned to beauty, and weeping was turned to laughter. All because of Jesus' faithful love for each of us, transforming us and empowering us to walk in His love.

When our boxing gloves come out, and they will (during NBA season), we must look to the Spirit to intervene and remind us what the battle is really about. One-upping your spouse? Keeping chores and workloads super fair? Punishing them for some way they hurt or disappointed us? Nope. You and your spouse are in a battle, alongside each other, to love one another as Christ loved the church.

With the Spirit's help, we show up to fight for our marriage, for our spouse. Without the Holy Spirit and without our spiritual armor, we'd never stand a chance. We have an enemy who hates the story God is writing for the world. An enemy who would delight in devastation and destruction reigning over every part of our lives.

When we know what we're up against, we can choose to lay down our weapons (or scorecards) and put on the spiritual armor we need for spiritual battle to love like Christ.

Love is a battlefield and it's not always pretty. But friends? Love's always the champion.

BE STRONG
in the Lord.

EPHESIANS 6:10

Draw it out:

1. Do you normally think of your marriage as a spiritual battlefield?

2. In difficulty or conflict, how do you think you could shift your mindset and remember your spouse is not your enemy?

3. What story does your marriage tell about God? What would you like it to say?

Pray together:

Praise God for the unsearchable riches of His love toward you both! Spend time confessing moments when you have walked in something other than His love toward your spouse. Ask the Holy Spirit for strength to engage the battle for love, dressed in the full armor of God.

Did I Marry the Wrong Person?

By J.D. Greear

> *Therefore, a man shall leave his father and mother and hold fast to his wife, and the two shall become one flesh. This mystery is profound, and I am saying that it refers to Christ and the church.*

EPHESIANS 5:31-32

We've all heard the "right person" myth: If you marry the right person, then your marriage is going to be happy. If your marriage is not happy, it's because you married the wrong person. I think my wife Veronica and I bought into this a little bit. We both had times, especially early in our marriage, where we thought, *Did I marry the wrong person?*

It didn't take us long—on our honeymoon, in fact—for us to realize two different people who approach life differently don't automatically become the same person when they get married.

For starters, we realized we're complete opposites with how we vacation. I need vacations to be planned, because, otherwise, you don't get the best reservations and you end up wasting your time. But if Veronica misses something, she's fine—as long as she is with her people and having a good time by a body of water.

At the core, Veronica is more "go with the flow;" I am more task-oriented. Not joking, I brought fourteen books on our honeymoon! I was in the middle of a PhD program and was thinking about getting stuff done. Meanwhile, Veronica just

wanted us to be together in the moment. I did get a lot of stuff done, but I wasn't present with my new wife.

While I probably shouldn't have taken fourteen books on our honeymoon, thankfully, we've both learned to appreciate how the other approaches life. It's been a bit of compromise and an ongoing process of learning to forbear with someone who does things differently. That takes a lifetime.

So even though my propensity to plan every second makes her crazy, we would've missed some amazing opportunities if I hadn't been such a planner. And I came to realize Veronica's willingness to just be with people was giving our family a relational dynamic we needed. God changed my perspective as I reflected on the fact that He makes each of us incomplete without other members of the body of Christ (see 1 Corinthians 12).

Many of us are used to thinking of the main purpose of marriage as companionship, and that is an important one. But it's also God's purpose to teach you to love somebody different. You're not loving the wrong person, because marriage is about learning to love a sinner the way God loves you.

Personally, I've found that when I put all the weight on the companionship of marriage, I'll be disappointed. But when I remember this other purpose of learning to love another weak human being, it helps you not just endure in marriage but learn to revel in the undeserved kindness she and I are getting to show and receive, just as I've received it from Christ. Any of us is never more like Christ than when we're loving somebody who doesn't quite deserve it in the moment.

My marriage is a unique opportunity to be a testimony to the power and beauty of Christ's kingdom. It's hard to talk about a gospel-centered marriage and not actually say what Paul himself said in Ephesians 5, that the mystery of marriage was created so that both roles proclaim the gospel in their own way. These roles were designed to reflect God's love and allow a marriage to flourish.

God assigned husbands the role of Christ-like leader, which means he is loving his wife like Christ loved the church, laying down his own interests for hers. He is responsible for setting the spiritual direction of the family.

God entrusts a wife with submitting to her husband the way the church submits to Christ. She's also designed to be the helper. God gave women a unique perspective so they can bring wisdom as chief counselors to their husbands. Submission is not inferiority; both men and women are made equally in the image of God but play different roles. Just like how God the Son is equal to God the Father, but while on Earth, He submitted to God the Father even though the two are equal and one.

In marriage, when each partner is playing their role, you see a beautiful demonstration of the gospel you can't see in any other relationship in the world.

Ultimately, all the things God has in my own life, including marriage, act as tools for making me more Christ-like. In marriage, you have to learn to love someone who is different and fallible. And they'll change. So if they're the right person today, they might not be the right person tomorrow. We're all sinners. To love like Christ loves, we aren't loving the "wrong" person, but we're loving a person who is sometimes wrong.

Draw it out:

1. Think about one way you and your spouse approach life differently. What have you learned from their way of doing things?

2. What is one unique way your spouse reflects the image of God?

3. What is one way you can trust God to help you show, through your marriage, the way He loves?

Pray together:

Reread Ephesians 5:31-32. Thank God for the mystery of marriage as a reflection of His rich love and grace. Take time to praise God for one unique quality He has given your spouse. Ask God to help you and your spouse grow in oneness and show the world the gospel by loving one another in your God-given differences.

Whatever, Wherever

By David and Meg Robbins

> *Then they answered Joshua, "Whatever you have commanded us we will do, and wherever you send us we will go."*

JOSHUA 1:16 (NIV)

When we got married, we kind of signed our lives away. Not in the way some may think when it comes to marriage. We signed a contract with the Lord, similar to what the Israelites said to Joshua in Joshua 1:16. We said, "Whatever you have commanded us we will do, and wherever you send us we will go." But early in our marriage, we didn't know exactly what *"whatever, wherever"* was going to look like.

At the time, we were living in suburbia and most of our neighbors were similar to us. Most of our friends and neighbors went to church, many to the same church we did. But at some point, we looked around and asked ourselves if this was really the life we said, *"whatever, wherever"* to. Was this really what we felt like we were signing up for and committing to with the Lord?

Those thoughts started a process of asking, *What is God asking us to be true in our lives? What do we hope and dream will be true in our lives?* We were pretty comfortable at the time, and we were thriving even with the sleepless realities of having three young kids. We decided to get away—just the two of us— and spend time thinking through these questions and coming up with joint values to guide us for the next season.

We considered our giftings, our passions, and the burdens (compassion for a particular issue or need) God had given us. And we asked Him, "How do you want us to steward this next season of our lives?"

We wrote everything down we could think of that felt important to us as we thought about the next three to five years. Nothing was off limits, not even the things we felt a little bit ashamed about writing down. We wrote down our values, processing things like homeownership versus renting, and job roles that focused on our individual strengths versus more collective contribution.

This is where our contract with the Lord came into play. Some of the things we would have ranked high ended up being pretty low when we considered being willing to do "whatever, wherever." We began to weed out and pray through our values, then decided the things we really wanted to be true of our family over the next few years. We found there were things that had felt really important but were ultimately blocking us from willingly embracing something different.

wherever
you send us,
WE WILL GO.

JOSHUA 1:16 (NIV)

We remember driving home from that hotel saying, "Our lives are about to radically change. We don't know what that means, where we're going, or exactly what we should do, but life is about to change in a major way."

At home, we sealed those values in a plastic, Ziploc bag. Yes, a Ziploc bag. And we began to pray over them daily. For six months we asked God to work in our hearts. During this time, He really drew us to Him and together toward oneness through total surrender of "*whatever, wherever*" He asked.

We had musings about where God was leading us, which got us excited as we thought about being together on the same team again, being on mission together. We'd been in a season where we were each doing totally different things in our work worlds, going in different directions. We wanted to sync up, flow together, and we wanted our family to be in a more diverse city center.

I (David) originally thought the next season was going to be in Miami. I was actually pretty determined that it needed to be Miami. Instead, it ended up being New York City, which felt totally overwhelming. But New York was where God wanted us to learn and be a part of His growing kingdom there. So, we sold our cars, bought a really big stroller for our kids, rented a 900 square-foot apartment, and found a public school much larger than our kids were accustomed to. Everything was new and our whole world kind of disassembled for a little bit.

But it ended up being the place where we were able to live out our top values and mission the most. It happened because of renewing our commitment to "whatever, whenever" in a new season. What ways has God already been working in your life and inviting you into a deeper surrender to Him? Have you shared those things with your spouse? God is worthy of our trust, even the "whatever, wherever" He asks of us.

Draw it out:

1. Do you and your spouse have shared values, goals, or a mission as a couple?

2. Spend some time alone to discuss, pray, and write down all the things that are most important for your life over the next five to ten years.

3. What are some of the things you both place a high value on and what excites you the most?

Pray together:

Thank God for creating each of you wonderfully and in a unique way. Thank Him for bringing you together to be a part of His growing kingdom. Ask Him to help you to submit your will to His will, your values to His values, and your lives to Him. Ask God to show you what this looks like, to mold your hearts and provide all you need to live this life and marriage on mission for Him.

Living and Leaving Your Legacy

By Dennis and Barbara Rainey

> *He established a testimony in Jacob and appointed a law in Israel, which he commanded our fathers to teach to their children, that the next generation might know them, the children yet unborn, and arise and tell them to their children, so that they should set their hope in God and not forget the works of God, but keep his commandments . . .*

PSALM 78:5-7

Not too long ago, our ten-year-old grandson was asked to describe each member of his family. He did a great job describing his siblings and parents. Some of it was pretty hilarious. And then, as I (Dennis) was about to leave, my son asked him, "How would you describe Papa?"

"Papa? He introduces people to God," he said.

I was totally unprepared for his answer. I don't know how a ten-year-old made that observation, but I thought, at that moment, I could die and be satisfied.

Study on the subject of leaving a legacy and impacting the next generation has led me to a very simple conclusion: We don't just *leave* a legacy. We *live* a legacy. When we live out our core values in front of our spouses, our children, our grandchildren, and a watching world, we model Jesus to them. We show them who Christ is to us. When they see that what we say matches up with what we do, it sticks.

That's what Jesus has called us to do. He's called us to model forgiveness, love, and what an authentic marriage looks like for our kids and grandkids. He's called us to live life with Him in such a way others can see and understand. Walking this earth as a human, He gave us a tangible example of how we could live.

I (Barbara) remember, when we first had kids, one of our biggest goals was to introduce them to God. I wanted them to know Him more than anything else — more than if they went to college, what they would do for a career when they grew up, what skills and talents they might develop, or even who they might marry one day. I knew, as sweet as they were, my kids were sinners, and they needed Jesus. I knew if they got their relationship with Jesus right, the rest would eventually fall into place.

Our marriages serve as models to the world of what real love can look like. For whatever reason, God chose to use the marriages of sinful human beings to paint a picture of His love for us. In the book of Ephesians, the Apostle Paul calls it a profound mystery, and it is. But a marriage that goes the distance is a living statement that God exists, that forgiveness is possible, and unconditional love is real. That's a big piece of the mystery a married couple represents to the planet. It's a picture of the relationship Christ has with His church—a picture people long for.

God created relationships. He knows how to make them work. This starts by submitting our lives to Christ and following Him, not just on Sunday morning, but every day. As Deuteronomy 6:7 envisions, we're to talk about our love for God and His commands "when you sit in your house, and when you walk by the way, and when you lie down, and when you rise." What we're really talking about here is living a life of integrity. Integrity is more than letting our yes be yes and our no be no (Matthew 5:37). It's also about living a life consistent with our beliefs, our words matching action. Integrity doesn't have to be flashy. It just has to be faithful. Integrity poses a constant struggle, but when it materializes, even a ten-year-old can tell what we're about. And that's a legacy worth living.

Draw it out:

1. What lessons is your life teaching others (both good or bad)?

2. Can people tell who Christ is by watching how you live?

3. How would you want future generations to describe you?

Pray together:

What areas in your life may be out of sync with your beliefs? Pray for wisdom and the strength to live a life of integrity. Pray that your actions — and your marriage — will show those around you something about who God is and what real love looks like. Ask Him to help you live the remainder of your days in a way that will impact future generations for His kingdom.

...SO THAT
THEY SHOULD

set

THEIR

hope

IN GOD...

PSALM 78:7

You Can Change Your Legacy

By Dave Wilson

A good man leaves an inheritance to his children's children...

PROVERBS 13:22

Marriage can be really hard.

We fail each other. We let each other down. We fall miserably short of meeting one another's needs. There are things we hope for and we don't get, but there are great reasons to stay in and fight for your marriage. Just one of those reasons is your legacy, the spiritual inheritance you'll leave to your kids... and their kids. That matters.

We had only been married for six months, but there Ann was ... screaming that marrying me was the biggest mistake of her life. Four months later, we were leading a marriage Bible study for college athletes. I kept thinking, *We can teach it, but we can't live it in our own home.*

It felt hopeless, like we weren't going to make it.

I came from a broken family that ended in divorce. I remember thinking, *I get to change this name. The Wilson name that was associated with alcoholism and adultery can now be associated with Jesus.* But I didn't realize it was going to require every ounce of everything I had, and have, to make my own marriage work. I just thought, *This is worth it. Whatever it costs I am willing to pay it. Let's do it.* I knew I had the chance to change my legacy.

But unresolved bitterness and anger began creeping into our marriage from my relationship with my dad. It came to a head one day, and Ann said to me, "You're going to have to forgive your dad."

I thought since I'm a pastor—I preach on this stuff!—it wouldn't take long. But it was a four- or five-year process. I had to walk through the anger and pain I thought I had resolved years ago, and allow the Holy Spirit to do the healing work. I couldn't have done it on my own. Again, many years stretched out before I got to a place of wishing him well and not wanting to punish him. But that decision to trust God and forgive my dad changed everything. It changed me as a husband, it changed me as a dad, and it changed my legacy.

Years later, I remember driving with my dad when he came to see me. I asked him, "Hey, Dad. Did you ever regret the divorce?" Before I could finish the question, he answered, "Yes."

I said, "You regretted it?"

He replied, "I missed out on your life. I missed out on your little brother's life." And I just remember thinking, *If he feels like that, I'm going to do whatever it takes to make my own marriage work.* And it took everything we had. We tried marriage conferences, mentoring, counseling . . . we did it all.

When marriage is hard, we always think it's not going to get better. It's hopeless. But we've seen it time and time again—in our marriage and in those around us. God renews, God restores, and God does miraculous things today. It's worth the fight.

Ann and I are now forty years in. When you fight through those valleys with each other and you get decades together, the intimacy is indescribable. It's worth fighting for that. (That's not to make any of you who have been divorced feel guilty or shamed. But the marriage you're in now, fight for it. Keep going.)

God has a bigger plan for your marriage than just you two being happy. You can mirror the steadfast love of God to other people. It's not that any of us reflect a perfect marriage (no one does!), because we're all broken people and mess up continually, but we continue to be needy for the God who saved us.

Ann's parents were married seventy years. Her dad started his own business and was super successful. He died at ninety-two, but in his last, probably ten years, he devoted his life to Ann's mom because she was struggling with Alzheimer's. Looking back, we don't think, "Wow. Look at that business he started." We think, "Wow. Look at the way he loved and cared for his wife. Well done."

Those are the things that matter.

God wants to use you with your flaws, your family history both good and bad, your brokenness, your gifts, your strengths, in your family, at your work, in your neighborhood. Wherever you are, He wants to use you. He has a purpose and plan for you, as a couple and as a family. You get the choice. Saying "yes" to God? That's a legacy worth leaving.

Draw it out:

1. If you could sum up your family of origin's legacy in a few sentences, what would you say?

2. How could God work with your past, your flaws, and any circumstance you're finding yourselves in to create in your lives a legacy that serves as an "inheritance" to your children?

3. Together, come up with two things you would want generations after you to say about your marriage.

Pray together:

Thank God for His goodness, forgiveness, and wisdom. Bring all the hurts of your past and insecurities about your future, both in your marriage and individual lives, before Him, knowing He is filled with compassion and love for you. Ask Him to bring to light anything that stops you from leaving a legacy that honors Him, and for the strength to make necessary changes with His help.

When Marriage Introduces You to the Gospel

By Lisa Lakey

> *In your hearts honor Christ the Lord as holy, always being prepared to make a defense to anyone who asks you for a reason for the hope that is in you; yet do it with gentleness and respect...*

1 PETER 3:15

We showed up on their doorstep young, in love, and unmarried. Not at all the lawfully wedded husband and wife they had been expecting. Still, they handed us keys to their rental home, twenty-five steps from their front porch.

It wasn't just happenstance that moved us next door to the Wilsons.

Our tenant/landlord relationship quickly morphed into a friendship between two couples fifty years apart in age. We shared meals, played cards, and even watered each other's plants when the other couple was away. Mrs. Wilson always had the right ingredients on hand to whip up a coconut cream pie from scratch at a moment's notice, because she knew it was my husband's favorite. Mr. Wilson once showed up on our doorstep in the pouring rain, umbrella in hand, to invite me to dinner. Josh was out of town, it was storming, and they didn't want me to be alone.

They loved us well with no agenda attached.

Even more than that, the way they interacted with one another was something I mentally noted every time we were together. Her loving attentiveness to her husband. The gentle way he spoke to her. The way they consulted each other on everything from dinner arrangements to finances. The obvious friendship they'd shared over decades of running businesses and a family, caring for loved ones, and enjoying each other's company. I had never seen anything like it. From watching them, I knew I wanted a marriage like the Wilsons'.

But even as a naïve, young, non-Christian woman, I picked up on something different. The Wilsons loved God in a way I had never seen. All this kindness, gentleness, and generosity pouring out of them? It was the straight-up love of Jesus. They didn't just go to church. They considered it an honor and privilege. We were often invited to tag along, but it was never a condition of the way they loved us.

By being loved by them and watching the way they loved God and each other, it made this once-twenty-something girl want to join them. They were introducing us to Jesus without us even knowing it, and they were presenting to us the allure of a marital commitment we hadn't yet made.

But there they were, twenty-five steps from our front porch.

The Wilsons became our stand-in grandparents, friends, and unintentional mentors. They shared their life with us, drawing us into their fold. They didn't expect perfection from us; they loved us like we were—broken parts, scars, and all—while showing us a different way. Through the Wilsons, I was introduced to the truth and beauty of the gospel.

Your marriage doesn't have to be perfect to have an eternal impact. Sometimes, it's those shared, raw moments of married life that unintentionally whisper to a hurting couple, "You're not alone." The way you cling to Jesus when absolutely nothing is seemingly going right, tenderly nudges their heart, "Perhaps there's hope for us, too."

Your
MARRIAGE
doesn't have to be
perfect
to have an
ETERNAL
IMPACT.

Even in struggles, both in their marriage and my own, I 've learned two things while watching the faithful couples around me:

1. Love is enduring.

Marriage is a long-game assignment. Not just because it's meant to last until "death do us part," but because you don't always see the fruit of the work you're putting in. Or from the prayers you've been saying for months, years maybe. But you make the choice to hold on because you see what this marriage could be. You trust God has a good plan, and you want a piece of it. So, you endure, and your love endures with every little choice you make to stay together.

2. Marriage is bigger than us.

A God-honoring marriage doesn't just impact the two imperfect people attempting to create a life together inside the four walls of their home. That's a limited view, and your marriage serves a limitless God. A God who can use your marriage to impact generations to come—your kids, your grandkids, your relatives, coworkers, all those in your sphere of influence . . . even the kid from down the street that makes himself at home in your house because even they can sense the safety of the enduring love of your marriage.

A marriage introduced me to the gospel. Not a sermon, book, TED talk, pamphlet left in my mailbox, or a TV evangelist promising miraculous healing with a gift of any amount. It was an open door, a comfy couch, and the occasional coconut cream pie.

A marriage on mission? It's as close as your front door.

Draw it out:

1. Have you witnessed a marriage that proclaims the gospel? What was it about their marriage that stood out to you?

2. How could your marriage—in its strengths *and* weaknesses—point others toward the love Christ has for His bride, the church?

Pray together:

Thank God that, even when your marriage is struggling, He can use it to point others toward Him. Confess to Him any doubts you have that your marriage could be used, and ask Him to open your eyes to those around you who could benefit from a comfy couch and friendship. Thank God for any marriages He has used to impact you, as well.

A Messy Masterpiece

By Brian Goins

> *Since then we have a great high priest who has passed through the heavens, Jesus, the Son of God, let us hold fast our confession. For we do not have a high priest who is unable to sympathize with our weaknesses, but one who in every respect has been tempted as we are, yet without sin. Let us then with confidence draw near to the throne of grace, that we may receive mercy and find grace to help in time of need.*

HEBREWS 4:14-16

We may never discover the identity of England-based, street-graffiti artist Banksy, but we know exactly where he's been. Whether he's tagged his art on bridges, billboards, or for you bacon lovers, on bodies of live pigs, people rush to post his statement-making pieces on their social feeds.

One of his more famous works, *Girl with Balloon*, went up for auction at Sotheby's in London. As the auctioneer's gavel slammed down, the auction house filled with a mysterious beeping emanating from the painting. Suddenly, the *Girl* descended into the elaborate golden frame where a secret shredder sliced half of the canvas into neat vertical strips.

A gape-mouthed buyer just spent $1.4 million for a tattered piece of art.

Originally, the graffiti artist wanted this "self-destruction" to make a statement against the inequality of art ownership.

Banksy staged "an attention-grabbing spectacle"—the shred-ding—" taking place within an attention-grabbing spectacle," the auction, "which highlighted through dark satire how art has become an investment commodity to be auctioned off to ultra-wealthy trophy-hunters."[3]

The scheme backfired. Three years later, nine bidders battled for ten minutes to claim the minced masterpiece. It sold for $25.4 million.

Turns out the art was worth more shredded.

In the art world, we ruthlessly protect our masterpieces. The absence of wear, restorations, and flaws ensure their value. Expose any piece to the forces of time, sunlight, and the elements, even priceless works of art can be devalued.

Much like how Banksy crafted a shredder in the frame of his artwork—living in a fallen world with broken humans will produce tears, rips, and scars. Maybe even make you feel devalued. Or maybe your marriage feels like it's been shredded.

You feel like you're sharing space with your spouse rather than sharing from your soul. Maybe you're locked in a battle of passive-aggressive one-upmanship. Or sarcasm has become your second language. Your spouse confessed to that same sin . . . again. Or maybe something from outside your marriage threatens your oneness. The child of promise turned into a prodigal child. The diagnosis didn't improve with treatment or prayer. The dream job turned into a corporate-downsizing nightmare.

Every marriage faces the sharp edges of broken people living in a fallen world.

But it seems like God has no problem exposing His art to the elements.

Take God's most treasured son, shredded for our benefit. Isaiah prophesied about Him, "But he was wounded for our transgressions, he was bruised for our iniquities: the chastisement of our peace was upon him; and with his stripes we are healed" (53:5, KJV.)

Later in the passage, Isaiah confounds us with this statement: "Yet it pleased the LORD to bruise him . . ." (53:10, KJV).

We don't serve a sadistic God who secretly enjoyed seeing His Son suffer. Instead, our all-knowing, unshackled by time God, can both feel the pain of loss and the joy from future victory.

"Out of the *anguish* of his soul he shall *see* and be satisfied; by his knowledge shall the righteous one, my servant, *make many* to be accounted righteous, and he shall bear their iniquities" (Isaiah 53:11, italics added).

God simultaneously anguished over His son's brutal suffering and rejoiced over what that pain produced: the salvation of many.

When we feel the sharp edges of brokenness, we don't have the luxury of seeing what our pain will produce. We only feel loss. We don't know if our spouse will change, our kids will return, or our circumstances will improve. But we know we serve a God who doesn't waste our sin, struggles, or failures. Though our own stripes won't secure salvation, they can point people to a Savior.

But he was *wounded* FOR OUR *transgressions...*

...and with his stripes

WE ARE HEALED.

ISAIAH 53:5 KJV

There's something refreshing about being in the presence of couples whose house feels more like a home than a museum; who laugh about how they made stupid decisions; who cry over the struggle they're facing; who talk freely about a divorce in the past and the principles they've applied to ensure this covenant lasts in the future; who tell the story of broken and restored trust.

When you encounter marriages that unapologetically display their flaws or share their pain, you long to know how they keep pursuing each other or where they found hope to go on. Inevitably, they point you back to the Divine Artist.

And they tell the story of how He took their mess and crafted a masterpiece.

Maybe you feel shredded right now. You're not alone. Your marriage is worth more because of the struggle. There's an Artist still at work.

Are you sharing your story?

Your marriage is God's messy masterpiece.

Draw it out:

1. What's hard about your marriage right now, or what challenges have you come through together?

2. Looking at any past challenges, can you now see God's divine hand working in your struggle?

3. What can others learn through your trials in marriage—either past challenges or current struggles?

Pray together:

Thank God for His unique design of marriage. Thank Him for not leaving us in our sins, weaknesses, and flaws, but using those to point a weary world toward Christ. Ask Him for help in removing any barriers to sharing your marriage journey with others—perfectionism, shame, embarrassment, or even just doubting anyone struggles with anything similar. And thank Him for working (He's still working!) to bring a masterpiece out of your mess.

Draw closer to others . . .

Way to go. We know prioritizing what matters most and focusing on a stronger, God-centered marriage isn't easy. But you did it anyway.

We're praying these fifty-two devotions have drawn you closer to God and each other. But what if the portrait He's painting is bigger than just the two of you? Find out how your marriage can impact others, and grab all the other offers in this book, by visiting us at FamilyLife.com/DrawnTogetherBonus.

Notes

1. Piper, John. "Love Her More and Love Her Less." DesiringGod. May 29, 1995. https://www.desiringgod.org/articles/love-her-more-and-love-her-less.

2. Benson, Kyle. "The Magic Relationship Ratio, According to Science." The Gottman Institute. https://www.gottman.com/blog/the-magic-relationship-ratio-according-science/

3. Edwards, Jonathan. "Banksy tried to destroy his art after it sold for $1.4 million. The shredded version just went for $25.4 million." The Washington Post. October 15, 2021. https://www.washingtonpost.com/nation/2021/10/15/shredded-banksy-painting/

Contributors

Leslie J. Barner is the chief of staff for FamilyLife. She is the author of numerous articles and several books and has overseen the development of numerous resources, including The Art of Marriage, Stepping Up, and Passport2Identity. Leslie and her husband, Aubrey, have four grown daughters and seven grandchildren. They reside in St. Cloud, Florida.

Jackie and Stephana Bledsoe are the founders of Happily-MarriedCouples. com, and have been featured on ABC News, The 700 Club, Moody Radio, YouVersion's Bible app, and Life-Way. Jackie is a podcast host, speaker, and author of *The 7 Rings of Marriage*. Stephana is a speaker, podcast host, encourager, and prayer intercessor for women of all ages. They have three amazing children whom they travel the world with ministering to families.

Janel Breitenstein is an author, freelance writer, speaker, and regular content contributor for FamilyLife. After five years in East Africa, her family of lives in Colorado, where they work on behalf of the poor with Engineering Ministries International. Her book, *Permanent Markers: Spiritual Life Skills to Write on Your Kids' Hearts*, empowers parents to creatively engage kids in vibrant spirituality. She and her hands-down best friend, John, have been married since 2000.

Candice Colclough and her husband Harold have a blended family in Little Rock. They have been married for ten years and have four children. Candice is currently an email marketing strategist for Cru and has contributed to blog posts for FamilyLife.com. The Colcloughs also host the *Marriage Stronger* podcast, focused on viewing the trials in marriage through the eyes of Christ.

Ron L. Deal is Director of FamilyLife Blended®, founder of Smart Stepfamilies™, and the author of the Smart Stepfamily Series of books, including the bestselling *Building Love Together in Blended Families: The 5 Love Languages®* and *Becoming Stepfamily Smart* (with Dr. Gary Chapman), *The Smart Stepfamily: 7 Steps to a Healthy Family*, and *Preparing to Blend*. Ron is a licensed marriage and family therapist, conference speaker, and host of the FamilyLife Blended podcast. He and his wife, Nan, have three sons and live in Little Rock, Arkansas.

Conway and Jada Edwards are both teachers, authors and leaders in the local church. Together, they planted One Community Church in Plano, Texas. Conway is the lead pastor and has a heart for discipling men and developing leaders. Jada serves as the Worship Arts Director and Women's Bible teacher and is committed to teaching women and students to know the Bible for themselves. Through their shared passion for singles and married couples, they have produced multiple books and resources to provide tools for healthy relationships.

Brian Goins and his wife, Jen, live in Melbourne, Florida, where Brian is the Senior Director of Strategic Projects and helps lead the Weekend to Remember team. He is also a producer of the documentary, "The Brain, The Heart, The World," a series exploring the dangers of pornography. The Goins have three kids: Brantley, Palmer, and Gibson. As a family they enjoy making annual treks to Montana to hike and ski and have loved attending Pine Cove family camp together.

Dr. Chris and Alisa Grace write, teach, and speak to couples, churches, and college students on healthy Christ-centered relationships. They are the co-directors of Biola University's Center for Marriage and Relationships, where Chris is a social psychologist/full professor and Alisa is an adjunct faculty member. Together they co-host *The Art of Relationships,* co-authored the *Marriage Mentoring Workbook and Video Series*, and serve on the speaking team for FamilyLife's Weekend to Remember.

Gayla Grace serves with FamilyLife Blended® and is passionate about equipping blended families as a writer and a speaker. She holds a master's degree in psychology and counseling and is the author of *Stepparenting With Grace: A Devotional for Blended Families* and co-author of *Quiet Moments for the Stepmom Soul*. Gayla and her husband, Randy, have been married since 1995 in a "his, hers, and ours" family. She is the mom to three young adult children and stepmom to two.

Derwin and Vicki Gray have been married over thirty years and have two adult children. In 2010, they founded Transformation Church (TC), a multiethnic, multigenerational, mission-shaped church near Charlotte, NC. A former NFL player, Derwin received his doctorate at Northern Seminary, and he is the author of several books, including the bestseller, *How to Heal Our Racial Divide*. Vicki is currently in graduate school at Wheaton College, pursuing an MA in Ministry Leadership.

J.D. Greear is the pastor of The Summit Church in Raleigh-Durham, NC, the author of several books including *Essential Christianity: The Heart of the Gospel in Ten Words* (2023) and the founder of J.D. Greear Ministries. He also is the pastor of *Summit Life*, a daily broadcast and weekly TV program, and the *Ask Me Anything* podcast. Pastor J.D. and his wife, Veronica, are raising four awesome kids.

Trent and Andrea Griffith serve at Cru and are speakers for FamilyLife's Weekend to Remember. Prior to joining Cru, Trent planted and pastored Gospel City Church in Granger, Indiana, for thirteen years. Trent and Andrea also spent fifteen years as conference speakers with Life Action Ministries. Trent is a graduate of Mid-America Baptist Theological Seminary in Memphis. Andrea graduated from Samford University in Birmingham, Alabama. Trent and Andrea have four children and live in Orlando, Florida.

D.A. and Elicia Horton have been married for twenty years and have three children. They serve at The Grove Community Church, where Elicia is Assistant Women's Ministry Director and D.A. an Associate Teaching Pastor. Elicia has a B.S. in Bible and Theology and Organizational Leadership (Calvary University) and two master's degrees in Organizational Development and Religious Studies (Calvary Theological Seminary). D.A. is an assistant professor at California Baptist University and has a Ph.D. in Applied Theology (SEBTS).

Daniel and Christina Im. Daniel is the Lead Pastor of Beulah Alliance Church, the author of multiple books, and a Gallup Strengths Performance Coach. Christina is a social worker, relationship coach, and Gottman 7 Principles leader, and is currently completing her Master's in Counseling Psychology degree. Together, they host the *IMbetween Podcast*, a podcast about marriage, parenting, faith, and everything in-between. Their passion is to give you the tools to build a strong, connected, and joy-filled marriage and family.

Aaron and Jamie Ivey live in Austin, Texas, where they parent four kids and do their best to change the world from right where they are. Jamie hosts "The Happy Hour with Jamie Ivey" podcast, and Aaron is a pastor and songwriter. The Iveys believe stories have a huge impact on the world, and they are honored to share stories in their books and from their co-hosted podcast "On the Other Side" with you.

 **Lisa Lakey** is the managing editor of digital content at FamilyLife. Before joining the ministry in 2017, she was a freelance writer covering parenting and Southern culture. She was also a contributing author to *The Story of Us: A Couples Devotional*. She and her husband, Josh, have been married since 2004. Lisa and Josh live in Benton, Arkansas, with their two children, Ella and Max.

 **Tracy Lane** is the manager of content strategy for FamilyLife. She is the author of numerous articles, coauthor of Passport2Identity, and a guest on multiple *FamilyLife Today®* broadcasts. Tracy and her husband, Matt, live in the Philadelphia suburbs with their three children. Follow her special needs motherhood journey at HeartForAnnie. Find her on instagram @HeartForAnnie.

 **Bob Lepine** is the on-air host for *Truth For Life*, and the former co-host of *FamilyLife Today*. He is the author of several books, including *Love Like You Mean It* and lives in Little Rock, Arkansas, with his wife, Mary Ann. They have five children. Bob also serves as an elder and teaching pastor at Redeemer Community Church. In 2022, he was inducted into the National Religious Broadcasters Hall of Fame.

 **Crawford and Karen Loritts** have four grown children and numerous grandchildren. Crawford has authored several books, is the senior pastor at Fellowship Bible Church in Roswell, Georgia, and hosts the *Living a Legacy* podcast. Karen is a teacher, mentor, and international speaker. She and Crawford coauthored two books, including *Your Marriage Today . . . And Tomorrow*.

 **Tim Muehlhoff** and his wife, Noreen, served with Cru for over thirty years. They are the proud parents of three adult sons. Tim has a Ph.D. in communication theory from the University of North Carolina at Chapel Hill. They currently serve at Biola University where Tim is a professor of communication studies and Noreen works in Student Development. Tim's weekly podcast, *Winsome Conviction* can be found at winsomeconviction.com.

 **Jonathan "J.P." Pokluda** is the Lead Pastor of Harris Creek Baptist Church in Waco, TX. He was formerly the leader of The Porch in Dallas, which grew to be the largest weekly young adult gathering of its kind in the country. JP's partner in ministry is Monica, his wife of seventeen years, and together they disciple their children, Presley, Finley, and Weston.

Dennis and Barbara Rainey are co-founders of FamilyLife. Barbara is the founder of EverThineHome.com, an online ministry to women and families. The Raineys were the hosts of the daily radio program *FamilyLife Today* for over twenty-six years. They focus on their family of six married children and twenty-seven grandchildren, while listening to the "laughter in the walls" as they sit by a cozy fire in their country home somewhere in Arkansas.

David and Meg Robbins are passionate about helping people integrate faith and family and equipping them to make a difference in their local communities. David became the President of FamilyLife in 2017. The Robbins have served together in a variety of ministry roles through the years, working primarily with the rising generation in Western Europe, Atlanta, and New York City. David and Meg, married in 2001, currently live in Orlando, Florida, with their four children.

Carlos Santiago is a senior writer for FamilyLife and has written and contributed to numerous articles, e-books, and devotionals. He was also a contributing author to *The Story of Us: A Couples Devotional*. He has a bachelor's degree in psychology and a master's degree in pastoral counseling. Carlos and his wife, Tanya, live in Orlando, Florida. You can learn more on their site, YourEverAfter.org.

Dr. Juli Slattery is a clinical psychologist, author, speaker, and the president/co-founder of Authentic Intimacy, a ministry devoted to reclaiming God's design for sexuality. Juli is passionate about helping Christians experience the fullness of God's gift of intimacy and sexuality. She is the author of twelve books, including *God, Sex, and Your Marriage* and the host of the weekly podcast *Java with Juli*. Juli and her husband Mike are the parents of three sons; they live in Akron, Ohio.

Ashford Sonii is a writer for FamilyLife. He enjoys ministry, learning, and communicating practical life applications of God's Word within marriage, family, and how to walk with Jesus. Ashford and his wife, Olivia, currently live in North Carolina with their twin girls, Ivey and Oakley.

Justin Talbert serves as the Student Pastor at Christ Community Church in Little Rock, Arkansas. He received his MDiv from Covenant Theological Seminary. Justin and his wife, May, have three sons: Soren, Aksel, and Isen. He loves reading fiction, writing non-fiction, and living somewhere in the middle.

 **Laura Way** lives with her husband, Aubrey, and their two vibrant daughters in Orlando, Florida. After living in East Asia for five years, relocating back to the States translated to two joyous years as a writer for FamilyLife. She currently works for Thirdmill.org spreading awareness for the lack of theological resources for the global church, and she writes (when the mood strikes) on her blog at hopeforthesojourn.com.

 **Dave and Ann Wilson** are the hosts of *FamilyLife Today*®. They are also cofounders of Kensington Church, a national, multicampus church that hosts more than 14,000 attendees every weekend. Since 1989, they have been featured speakers at FamilyLife's Weekend to Remember and have also hosted their own marriage conferences across the country. The Wilsons live in the Detroit area and have three grown sons, CJ, Austin, and Cody, as well as three daughters-in-law and six grandchildren.

LET'S KEEP THE

conversation

GOING

Continue giving your marriage the intentionality it deserves.

Join FamilyLife for three days of romance and reconnection with your spouse at a Weekend to Remember. With locations all over the country, get away or stay close to home for a weekend of:

 Biblically based insights from top speakers and marriage experts.

 Relaxing time alone together, free from distractions.

 Helpful tools and resources for an immediate impact on your marriage.

Head to weekendtoremember.com to register!

FamilyLife.
A Cru Ministry

Pursue what matters most

At FamilyLife, we get it.

Every home is full of moments scattered and sacred, heart-pounding and hilarious, messy and marvelous.

But we believe God's Word has real wisdom for real families. We help your family push through the days that are hectic and heart-wrenching—to come together in spite of the hard.

Through resources and experiences, we'll help you connect in ways that count with those you love.

Lean on us, laugh with us, learn with us, and walk with us to pursue the relationships that matter most.

Find out how we can help your family grow together at FamilyLife.com.